EVERTON'S

Z-STARS

★★★★★★★★★

THE MEN WHO MADE HISTORY. 1984-1987

Compiled by KEN ROGERS

featuring
HOWARD KENDALL
– inside the dressing room

SPORT MEDIA
A Trinity Mirror publication

Published in Great Britain in 2004 by:
Trinity Mirror Sport Media,
PO Box 48, Old Hall Street,
Liverpool L69 3EB

Executive Editor: KEN ROGERS
Art Editor: RICK COOKE
Publishing Executive: DAN WILLOUGHBY

ISBN 0-9546871-0-8

Printed and bound by Biddles Ltd.

Contents

Foreword

EVERTONIANS are amongst the country's most passionate fans. Whenever they gather together one thing is guaranteed to fire up the emotions . . . the stirring sound of "Z-Cars" as the players step into that legendary Goodison arena. When I was considering the title options for this very special book about the most successful era in the history of the club, that distinctive piece of theme music leapt into my mind.

"Z-Cars" fittingly became "Z-Stars" as a publication began to take shape that is all about the men who made history in those famous royal blue shirts under the astute guidance of the most successful Everton manager of all time, Howard Kendall.

As a sports writer and later Sports Editor of the Liverpool Echo, I was fortunate enough to work closely with Howard throughout the glorious Eighties. Indeed, many of the match reports I penned at that time – including legendary games like the taming of Bayern Munich at Goodison – are now part of Everton history. They tell the story of a four-year rush for silverware that brought the Championship twice, the FA Cup and the European Cup Winners Cup to Goodison Park. I would like to thank former Echo colleagues like Ian Hargraves and Ric George whose reports also form part of this book.

"Z-Stars" has a clear structure. Every season between 1983/84 and 1986/87 has an introduction that sets the scene. This is followed by a series of carefully selected match reports that will evoke powerful memories for the Evertonians who followed the Blues home and away at that time. Those reports highlight the qualities of inspirational heroes like Peter Reid, Andy Gray, Graeme Sharp, Neville Southall, Kevin Sheedy, Trevor Steven, Kevin Ratcliffe and the rest.

Alongside the reports come the images from the unmatchable archive of the Liverpool Daily Post & Echo, every picture a reminder of the achievements of the "Z-Stars" super heroes.

Behind every match report is a very special "Inside The Dressing Room" analysis from the man himself – Howard Kendall. To say that it was a joy to sit down with Howard again and discuss the key matches, the astute and inspirational signings he made and some of the secrets and stories from behind the scenes is an understatement. We had many enjoyable sessions together during the production of this book and his love for Everton – a marriage he once called it – is unquestionable. I would like to thank him for his tremendous support and co-operation in helping to piece together the "Z-Stars" story.

I would also like to pay one final tribute to Colin Harvey whose coaching skills and Evertonian heart helped to work the magic alongside the legendary Mr Kendall. What a team - on and off the pitch.

– Ken Rogers

Howard Kendall would like to dedicate his input into this book to the players who were the heartbeat of the Eighties and to every Blues' fan who helped inspire the most successful era in Everton Football Club's history. A special tribute also goes to a dear friend, coach Mick Heaton, who died in tragic circumstances.

83/84
Howard's revolution

IT BEGAN WITH A WINTER OF DISCONTENT AND LEAFLETS HANDED OUT CALLING FOR THE MANAGER AND THE CHAIRMAN TO QUIT.
IT ENDED WITH TWO WEMBLEY APPEARANCES AND A CLUB DRIVING FORWARD WITH PRIDE AND PASSION.
THIS IS WHERE THE FOLKLORE OF '84 TO '87 BEGAN WITH A MILK CUP AND THEN AN FA CUP CHALLENGE THAT WOULD BE THE CATALYST TO LAUNCH EVERTON FOOTBALL CLUB TOWARDS THE MOST SUCCESSFUL PERIOD IN ITS LONG AND DISTINGUISHED HISTORY. . .

THE 1983/84 season was the definitive season of change and challenge. Having finished seventh in the table the previous year, an improvement of one place on Howard Kendall's opening 1981/82 campaign, there was obviously a lot of focus on the manager's third full year at the helm.

Harry Catterick had appeared almost untouchable for over a decade before stepping aside in 1973, but successive Everton managers had come under close scrutiny at the end of their third year at the helm. Billy Bingham was sacked five months into his fourth. Gordon Lee also only managed three full seasons, although he was given marginally more time than his predecessor.

HOWARD KENDALL: He had a "love affair" with Everton

Kendall was realistic enough to know that he would also be under the microscope as his third season dawned and the way things started for the Blues, the manager's future was looking anything but secure. Everton failed to score in seven of their opening 15 League matches which included home defeats against West Ham, Luton Town and Norwich City and reversals at Ipswich, Leicester, Liverpool and Arsenal.

The Blues had looked anything but convincing in disposing of Chesterfield in the opening round of the Milk Cup in the October and by the time Coventry City came to Goodison Park for a third round clash on November, 9, 1983, the fans were beginning to vote with their feet. The attendance was a painfully low 9,000 and this was not the bright new world that Kendall had planned for the club he had graced as an outstanding player.

It is now part of Goodison folklore what happened that night. People talk about Oxford United in the fifth round being the day that Everton's Eighties renaissance began. The truth is that the Coventry clash was much more significant.

During the Chesterfield game in the previous round some supporters had handed out leaflets declaring: "30,000 stay-away fans can't be wrong. Kendall and Carter out."

It was against this background of discontent that the Coventry game took place. However, chairman Philip Carter was steadfast in his belief that change would be disastrous for the Blues at that moment in time. Everton owe Carter a lot for his firm leadership as that 1983-84 season began to unfold. But with those leaflets still in the hands of an increasingly disgruntled and worried fan base, it was crucial that Kendall and his players pulled something out of the bag against Coventry.

Who knows what would have happened if Everton had lost against the Sky Blues. Let's put it this way. Football history can swing one way or the other on one game, one blunder, one dodgy back pass, one glorious goal, and one absolutely crucial result.

I well remember the final three paragraphs of my Echo match report that November evening . . .

"The 9,000 faithful who had turned out on a cold and uninviting night had finally been given their reward. They will still reflect on that worrying first half when Coventry had far too much of their own way, Neville Southall being forced to make vital saves from Bamber and Hendrie.

"But in that late revival, we saw a glimpse of the skill and determination that inspired Kendall to pay £700,000 for record signing Adrian Heath. He is a tremendous little character who knows that his impact has not been as great as he would have hoped.

"But the ability is there and now Everton must begin to believe in themselves again. Their problems are far from over, but this victory has given them breathing space."

Breathing space indeed. We all took a deep breath that night, including the man in the hot seat. Howard Kendall's dream was still alive and kicking. The 9,000 didn't know it as they left the stadium, but they had just been in on the start of what would become the most successful four years in Everton's history.

LIFE SAVER: Graeme Sharp (hidden) heads home against Coventry to take Everton into the last 16 of the Milk Cup

The Match...

BATTLING BLUES FIND AN EXTRA SHARP FINALE

EVERTON 2   COVENTRY 1
Milk Cup, Third Round, November 9, 1983

Everton(4-4-2): Southall, Harper, Bailey, Ratcliffe, Higgins, Steven, Irvine, Heath, Sharp, King, Sheedy. Sub: Reid.
Coventry (4-4-2): Suckling, Roberts, Gynn, Grimes, Peake, Allardyce, Bennett, Hunt, Bamber, Hendrie, Platneur. Sub: Singleton.
Referee: Mr A Challinor (Maltby).
Goals: Bamber (50) 0-1; Heath (78) 1-1; Sharp (90) 2-1.
Conditions: Cool evening, pitch excellent.
Bookings: Ratcliffe (Everton), Allardyce and Bamber (Coventry).
Attendance: 9,080.

By Ken Rogers

EVERTON came storming back from the brink of disaster last night, thrilling the Goodison Park faithful with a grandstand finish that sent battling Coventry City tumbling out of the Milk Cup.

Graeme Sharp snatched a sensational winner in the dying seconds of the game after brilliant work on the right by Adrian Heath. The crowd gave the players a standing ovation as they strode from the pitch, applause that must have been music to the ears of manager Howard Kendall.

The sheer elation that followed this 2-1 third round win empha- sised the importance of this success to Kendall and his players.

They have been under mounting pressure in recent weeks, the tension showing itself clearly in the first half when the Blues lacked the confidence and conviction to shake a Midlands side that had won three away games on the trot.

When the towering Dave Bamber nodded home a 50th minute opener for Coventry it looked distinctly grim for the Blues.

The game was transformed from the moment that Everton made a 69th minute substitution, Trevor Steven coming off to be replaced by Peter Reid. The Blues were to suddenly find a new gear, creating a bundle of chances that had the visitors clinging on desperately to their one goal lead.

Alan Irvine did well to provide Mark Higgins with a clear heading opportunity in the box, but the Goodison skipper couldn't believe it when his effort rebounded back off the foot of the post. Heath then fired in a superbly struck left-foot shot that brought the best out of Coventry's talented young keeper Perry Suckling.

Sharp cut loose from the right of the box, only for Suckling to pull off yet another excellent stop. With the tension and the excitement mounting, Everton finally breached the Coventry rearguard after 78 minutes.

Sharp did well to win the ball at the far post, injuring himself as he turned it back into a packed goalmouth. Higgins and Andy King had shots blocked and when it seemed that the ball would never go in, Heath finally struck the decisive blow from close range to make it 1-1.

The relief that swept down from the terraces completely enveloped the players who were suddenly gripped with the belief that this tie was there for the taking.

The drama was far from over and five minutes from time Everton almost paid a heavy price for their all-out efforts to grab the winner. As the Blues flung men forward they were suddenly caught out by a long run from the halfway line by defender Micky Gynn. He homed in on the box with only Neville Southall to beat.

To Everton's relief the Welsh international goalkeeper pulled off an instinctive save with his feet and the Goodison men were able to sweep back quickly on the offensive.

The goal opened up for Irvine after good approach play by Heath, but the midfield man somehow headed wide of the target. The seconds ticked away and as the clock reached the 90 minute mark it seemed that the tie was heading for a Highfield Road replay.

But Irvine, battling to make amends for his miss, struck a superb crossfield ball towards Heath on the right. The forward did magnificently to get in his cross under pressure and Sharp's close range header was almost sucked into the net by the Gwladys Street fans.

The 9,000 faithful who had turned out on a cold and uninviting night had finally been given their reward. They will still reflect on that worrying first half when Coventry had far too much of their own way, Southall being forced to make vital saves from Bamber and Hendrie.

But in that late revival we saw a glimpse of the skill and determination that inspired Howard Kendall to pay £700,000 for record signing Heath. He is a tremendous little character who knows that his impact has not been as great as he would have hoped.

But the ability is there and now Everton must begin to believe in themselves again. Their problems are far from over, but this victory has given them the breathing space.

 STAR MAN

At half time my two contenders for the Everton man-of-the-match award were John Bailey and Neville Southall.

The full-back was playing with tremendous determination and the keeper had demonstrated his undoubted ability on more than one occasion.

But by the end of the 90 minutes I had to go for Adrian Heath. He scored the equaliser and bubbled to life, showing skill and commitment to lay on Graeme Sharp's winner.

HOWARD KENDALL
– inside the dressing room

People always ask me what was the real turning point for us in that eventful 1983/84 season in which disaster stared us in the face one moment and cup glory beckoned the next. The famous Oxford United game in the fifth round of the Milk Cup in January, 1984 is often touted as the great turning point for us. Everyone remembers Adrian Heath's lifesaving late strike on the ice at the Manor Ground, Oxford, and how it kept alive a cup dream that would ultimately lead us to that first ever Wembley clash between Everton and Liverpool.

I've thought about it a lot, but it has an obvious rival. The third round clash with Coventry City at Goodison in early November, 1983 was at least as significant, possibly more so. That was the night when a Graeme Sharp winner in the dying moments turned a possible nightmare into a victory that gave me particular satisfaction. In the previous round leaflets had been handed out by a small group of people demanding that both chairman Philip Carter and myself should quit.

There was clearly discontent amongst the supporters at that time. The fact that less than 9,000 turned up at Goodison for that Coventry tie highlights how disappointing we had been in the early part of that season. The fans voiced their displeasure by not turning up and the rest made it absolutely clear that things were just not good enough.

Those leaflets were planned and printed by a small minority, but the action would have taken on a whole new significance if we had lost that night. We knew we had to win or those people may have got their own way. I recall there was a determination in the lads to put things right.

Obviously there is a massive responsibility on the manager to select the right team for a particular challenge. I left Peter Reid on the bench for that Coventry clash and it nearly rebounded on me. Looking back, you realise that you can't have influential people like Reidy sitting on the sidelines, especially when the going is getting tough which it clearly was at that time. You need your battlers in the thick of the action. I realised that later, but before the game you assess the tactics and believe you are doing the right thing. Peter had a major influence when we eventually launched him into the fray. I was so pleased with his attitude. I realised against Coventry that he was going to be a key player in our fight to make further progress. He was virtually ever-present after that.

I thought about the leaflet episode as I left Goodison that night. We had finally given the fans something to shout about. I told myself that it was only a small minority who had been involved, but the whole business could have been very dangerous if we had lost the tie.

And so when I think about the real turning point, almost certainly it was that Milk Cup win over Coventry. It shows you what a narrow line it can be between success and failure. The following day I went out and signed Andy Gray and also decided to promote Colin Harvey to first team coach. We went on to enjoy the most successful period in the history of Everton Football Club.

INCHY POWER: The commitment was never in doubt. Adrian did us proud in the Eighties

The Match...

INCHY'S ICE DANCE AT OXFORD

OXFORD UNITED 1 EVERTON 1
Milk Cup, Fifth Round, January 18, 1984

Oxford United: Hardwick, Hinshelwood, McDonald, Train, Briggs, Shotton, Lawrence, Biggins, Vinter, Hebberd (Whatmore 18), Brock.
Everton: Southall, Stevens, Harper, Ratcliffe, Mountfield Reid, Irvine, Heath, Sharp. Johnson (Richardson 70), Sheedy.
Referee: J. Hunting (Leicester).
Goals: McDonald (68) 1-0; Heath (81) 1-1.
Conditions: Cold evening, pitch hard and icy.
Booking: Irvine for foul on Hebberd.
Attendance: 14,333.

By Ken Rogers

OXFORD UNITED looked set to add another famous scalp to their Milk Cup battle honours last night when a blundering back pass nine minutes from time let Everton off the hook.

The Third Division outfit - giant-killers over Leeds, Newcastle and Manchester United - were leading 1-0 and looking full value for their slender advantage when young winger Kevin Brock panicked under pressure from Peter Reid. He played a suicide ball towards his own goal area and Adrian Heath was on it like a flash.

The Everton man skipped around goalkeeper Hardwick and curled his shot inside the post. It was a crucial strike - matching his memorable equaliser against Coventry in the third round - and the home side were left cursing their misfortune on a night when they had suffered a major injury blow and still managed to carve out the best of the chances.

With just 18 minutes on the clock, Alan Irvine slid in to a 50-50 challenge on Trevor Hebberd and the Oxford player stayed down in considerable pain. He was stretchered off and Irvine was booked by referee John Hunting,

Neil Whatmore, the former Bolton striker, was thrust into the action on a hard and icy pitch that was to prove extremely tricky for both sets of players.

Oxford had a livewire customer on the right wing in George Lawrence, a man who was to have an outstanding match and wage an intriguing battle with Gary Stevens.

The young Blues' defender, back after injury, had switched flanks to replace the injured John Bailey with Alan Harper taking the right-back role.

Oxford were determined to secure the important early break-through and they took advantage of the famous Manor Ground slope to test Neville Southall after 16 minutes, the keeper going down quickly to turn away a Gary Briggs header.

At the other end Peter Reid gave Kevin Sheedy a clear shooting chance, Hardwick parrying a solid shot that was to prove Everton's only real opportunity of the half.

Oxford, playing their 39th game of the season, were the dominating force with Steve Biggins heading wide and Southall saving brilliantly from Lawrence on the stroke of half time.

The Blues had moved David Johnson up front alongside Graeme Sharp. He was to have a quiet night, eventually coming off 20 minutes from time after Oxford had snatched the lead.

Brock had lofted in a dangerous free-kick from the left that was turned back across goal by Briggs. Former Manchester City defender Bobby McDonald had pushed forward to flick out his left foot and steer a shot beyond Southall.

McDonald scored a crushing double against Everton in an FA Cup quarter-final replay in March, 1981. It looked as if he was going to be celebrating another match winner with the Blues becoming another impressive Oxford statistic.

But substitute Kevin Richardson came on to battle and prompt

in midfield and Heath moved up front to provide a livelier edge.

Brock's momentary lapse - the only blemish on a stylish perform-ance - was to stun the home fans as Heath went on his little ice dance, scoring maximum points for style and execution.

Everton's back four were forced to battle away against a determined Oxford with Derek Mountfield and Gary Stevens both playing their part. But the Everton man-of-the-match had to go to Adrian Heath for that excellent equaliser and a busy display that earned the Blues a replay.

HOWARD KENDALL
– inside the dressing room

Some people say Adrian Heath's late equaliser saved my job. You can walk a tightrope in football and things can go either way. Either you fall or you reach the other side and power on.

I remember the Manchester Evening News running a poll when Alex Ferguson was going through a difficult time early on. The end product was a headline saying that Fergie must go! It's interesting to think what would have happened if the United board had listened.

That moment at Oxford was all the more tantalising because the pitch was icy and tricky at the end where Inchy scored. People criticised Brock for his backpass, but people don't appreciate the pressing of Peter Reid that led to the error.

Heath was alert to what was going on and knew that Reidy would put tremendous pressure on the defender. The goal was a crucial one. Would I have been sacked if he had missed? I like to think that the Everton board - like the United board - would have been strong at an important moment.

That's what football is all about. History can be made around one decision.

REPLAY PUNCHLINE:
Adrian Heath's dramatic late equaliser at Oxford set the scene for an emphatic 4-1 replay success at Goodison with goals from Heath, Richardson, Sharp and Sheedy. It meant the Blues had claimed the Milk Cup scalps of Chesterfield, Coventry, West Ham and Oxford. Aston Villa were now the only hurdle to a trip to Wembley and a 2-0 semi-final, first leg result, with goals from Sheedy and Richardson, set things up perfectly. The return at Villa Park was to prove extremely tense, not least when the home side pulled one back, ironically through a man who the following decade would actually become an Everton FA Cup Final hero – Paul Rideout.

However, nothing was going to stop Howard Kendall's men marching on towards an historic Wembley Final against arch-rivals Liverpool.

MERSEYPRIDE: The Everton and Liverpool players together on a Wembley stage

The Match...

MERSEYPRIDE UNDER TWIN TOWERS

EVERTON 0 LIVERPOOL 0
Milk Cup Final, March 25, 1984

Everton: Southall, Stevens, Bailey, Ratcliffe, Mountfield, Reid, Irvine, Heath, Sharp, Richardson, Sheedy (Harper 75).
Liverpool: Grobbelaar, Neal, A. Kennedy, Lawrenson, Whelan, Hansen, Dalglish, Lee, Rush, Johnston (Robinson 90), Souness.
Referee: Mr A. Robinson (Portsmouth).
Conditions: Persistent rain; pitch soft.
Booking: Souness (41) for foul on Heath.
Corner count: Liverpool 10 Everton 3.
Attendance: 100,000. Receipts: £670,000.

By Ken Rogers

MERSEYSIDE claimed a magnificent Milk Cup victory at Wembley yesterday.
In a goalless but unforgettable final, English soccer's greatest rivals did themselves proud - both on and off the pitch. To use Bill Shankly's famous old saying, it would have been a "travesty of justice" if either Liverpool or Everton had lost this match.

The Blues will reflect on an inspired first half in which they proved beyond any doubt that in terms of determination and commitment they can stand shoulder to shoulder with the Cup holders. Everton were certainly not overawed by the occasion and were denied what looked like a blatant penalty after six minutes.

The Reds, using their vast experience, turned the tide in the second half when Ian Rush in particular had golden opportunities to make it four Milk Cup victories on the trot for the Anfield men.

But the 35-goal striker was left cursing both his own luck and the brilliance of Welsh international team-mate Neville Southall, who is undoubtedly one of the top keepers in Britain at the moment.

The game went into 30 minutes of extra time, a familiar Wembley experience for Liverpool, but at the end of the day it was honours even with a replay scheduled for Maine Road on Wednesday.

The Everton fans knew that their side would have to play to the very peak of their form to match a Liverpool outfit fresh from that emphatic European Cup victory against Benfica in midweek. In that respect skipper Kevin Ratcliffe had a storming game in the heart of the defence, while John Bailey was another player who not only defended well but also used the ball to tremendous effect down that left channel.

It was a typical forward ball from the experienced full-back that led to the controversial penalty incident after six minutes when Heath claimed that Alan Hansen had blocked a goalbound shot with his hand. Sharp had flicked on Bailey's long ball with Heath sliding in on goalkeeper Bruce Grobbelaar in an effort to make a decisive touch.

Heath was on the floor, but he managed to scoop the ball towards the net. It struck Hansen's knee and then his hand, but to Everton's total disbelief referee Alan Robinson waved play on. The Reds' camp later claimed it was unintentional on Hansen's part, but the crux of the matter was that the shot was clearly heading for the net and Heath was right to feel cheated of a sensational opener. Almost immediately, Liverpool had another let-off when Kevin Richardson drilled in a left foot volley that glanced the wrong side of the upright with the midfield man already turning away in celebration with his arm in the air.

It was the confident start that Everton boss Howard Kendall had called for to give his side a chance against their famous rivals.

It was understandable that Joe Fagan pulled no punches in his half time team talk and the Reds certainly looked a different proposition in the second half when Alan Kennedy, Kenny Dalglish and Rush all went desperately close to breaking the deadlock. Liverpool had emerged after the break full of determination with Kennedy taking off on a long and winding run that took him to the edge of the Blues' box. Space opened up in front of the full-back, but he was on his wrong foot and screwed a shot wide of the post.

As the Reds continued to surge forward Ronnie Whelan set up a fine chance for Rush that brought the very best out of Southall who was forced to make a point blank save.

Everton had brought on substitute Alan Harper for Kevin Sheedy who was feeling an earlier injury and as the teams turned round for extra time, Fagan sent on a fresh pair of legs in the shape of Michael Robinson who replaced the tiring Craig Johnston.

The impeccable Southall pushed out a stunning volley from Rush.

Whelan finally had the ball in the net, but was ruled offside, and in the last bid for victory his team-mate Kennedy was also denied an opener. Rush had made a powerful break from the halfway line before setting up the chance for the full-back, but a linesman's flag once again signalled the narrowest of offside decisions.

As the noise all round the stadium reached a deafening crescendo, referee Robinson finally brought to an end to one of the most exciting finals for many years.

 **STAR MAN**

Everton had outstanding contenders for their man-of-the-match award. Peter Reid turned it on in the first half. John Bailey used all his experience to produce a superb display at left-back, but the vote went to skipper Kevin Ratcliffe who was an inspiring figure from start to finish in the heart of the defence.

HOWARD KENDALL
– inside the dressing room

Shortly before that famous Milk Cup Final at Wembley we had met Liverpool in the League at Goodison Park and secured a 1-1 draw with a goal from Alan Harper who was naturally thrilled to score against his former club. It meant we had gone eight games unbeaten and confirmed that our improvement was not restricted to continued progress in the two domestic Cup competitions. We were finally beginning to build something very special and that league draw at Goodison gave our fans a big lift. We had already gained more than a bit of pride by securing our Wembley place after a two-legged semi-final victory over Aston Villa.

The Milk Cup run had been a hard slog. The opening round was also a two-legged affair with Chesterfield our opponents and while Graeme Sharp gave us a 1-0 lead at their place, the lower league side fought hard at Goodison in the return. It ended up 2-2 with Adrian Heath and Trevor Steven on the mark for us. Sharpy's away strike proved the difference.

I've already talked about the 2-1 win over Coventry in the third round. We then beat West Ham over two games before the fateful clash at Oxford, again featured earlier. We romped home in the replay at Goodison, scoring four times with a curtain of snow hanging across the stadium. It seemed that nothing was going to stop us in our quest for Wembley and while Villa ran us close in the semi-final, fate was dictating that Merseyside's two football giants would meet for the first time under the famous Twin Towers.

We were making history. The clubs would subsequently meet on several occasions at Wembley during the decade. I recall that a unique joint team photograph was taken at Bellefield in 1986. It was the first time that Everton and Liverpool players had posed together for a formal team picture, red then blue standing shoulder to shoulder. I well remember the day. There had been some discussion about which training ground should be used. It was a pride thing, but it was also about logistics. In the end, Kenny Dalglish agreed that they should come to us. It was blowing a gale and everyone was freezing cold, but we couldn't reorganise it and so everyone had to grin and bear it.

However, the image was a special one and it symbolised the mood of Merseyside at that time. It also highlighted the fact that Liverpool, as a city, is different to most of the other big soccer centres. That was highlighted perfectly when the Milk Cup Final brought us together for the first time at Wembley on March 25, 1984.

Supporters travelled down together. You'd see a car with a blue scarf hanging out of one window and a red one out of the other. It was the same with the coaches on the motorway, and the trains. There was no segregation. No need. We're better than that. We are probably more passionate and more partisan than anyone when it comes to defending the interests of our clubs, but Evertonians and Liverpudlians can drink together and laugh together as well. That's what makes us so special and it's something we should work hard at to retain, despite the fact that there have been bits and pieces of problems at derbies in subsequent years.

What I remember most about that Wembley game was the hand-ball of Hansen. I never let Alan forget it when I see him. Evertonians have got the incident imprinted on their minds. Adrian Heath's drive first hit the defender's knee, but it was still goal-bound until he scooped it away with his left hand. No doubts. No arguments. Everyone in the stadium saw it - except the referee. It's amazing how often that seems to happen in a game. You get 40,000, or in this case 100,000, certain of what they've seen. The only one with the blinkers on is the referee!

Some might say that official Alan Robinson's decision was equal to that of Clive Thomas in 1977 when Bryan Hamilton had a famous semi-final goal disallowed at Maine Road, also against Liverpool.

Possibly it wasn't. Thomas seemed to invent a decision on that occasion. In this case, I felt Robinson just bottled it. I suppose you could argue that the draw sent everyone home happy. The blue and red scarves were able to fly side by side again on the journey back.

Don't get me wrong. It was a great day. The chants of "MERSEY-SIDE" that roared round the stadium made us all feel ten feet tall. But I would have preferred the final chant to have been a royal blue one. A Graeme Souness goal separated us in the replay at Maine Road. They had the Cup, but we definitely had our pride and another challenge to look forward to, this time in the FA Cup. There is no doubt that Liverpool were football's number one team at that point. Suddenly we had demonstrated that we could live with them and match them.

After the way the season had started, this was a major step forward and I knew that Everton Football Club was finally on the march.

YOU'RE HAVIN' A LAUGH: Peter Reid and Alan Kennedy share a joke

1983/84 MILK CUP STATS, ROUND BY ROUND:

Home in bold

ROUND	DATE	TEAM	RESULT
2	Oct 4	Chesterfield	W 1-0 Sharp
	Oct 26	**Chesterfield**	D 2-2 Heath, Steven
3	**Nov 9**	Coventry C.	W 2-1 Heath, Sharp
4	Nov 30	West Ham	D 2-2 Reid, Sheedy
R	**Dec 6**	**West Ham**	W 2-0 King, Sheedy
5	Jan 18	Oxford U.	D 1-1 Heath
R	**Jan 24**	**Oxford U**	W 4-1 Heath, Richardson, Sharp, Sheedy
SF	**Feb 15**	**Aston Villa**	W 2-0 Richardson, Sheedy
	Feb 22	Aston Villa	L 0-1
F*	Mar 25	Liverpool	D 0-0
R+	Mar 28	Liverpool	L 0-1

* Final at Wembley
+ Replay at Maine Road

1983/1984 ENGLISH DIVISION 1 TABLE

	P	HW	HD	HL	HGF	HGA	AW	AD	AL	AGF	AGA	PTS	GD
Liverpool	42	14	5	2	50	12	8	9	4	23	20	80	+41
Southampton	42	15	4	2	44	17	7	7	7	22	21	77	+28
Nottm Forest	42	14	4	3	47	17	8	4	9	29	28	74	+31
Man Utd	42	14	3	4	43	18	6	11	4	28	23	74	+30
QPR	42	14	4	3	37	12	8	3	10	30	25	73	+30
Arsenal	42	10	5	6	41	29	8	4	9	33	31	63	+14
Everton	42	9	9	3	21	12	7	5	9	23	30	62	+2
Tottenham	42	11	4	6	31	24	6	6	9	33	41	61	-1
West Ham	42	10	4	7	39	24	7	5	9	21	31	60	+5
Aston Villa	42	14	3	4	34	22	3	6	12	25	39	60	-2
Watford	42	9	7	5	36	31	7	2	12	32	46	57	-9
Ipswich	42	11	4	6	34	23	4	4	13	21	34	53	-2
Sunderland	42	8	9	4	26	18	5	4	12	16	35	52	-11
Norwich	42	9	8	4	34	20	3	7	11	14	29	51	-1
Leicester	42	11	5	5	40	30	2	7	12	25	38	51	-3
Luton	42	7	5	9	30	33	7	4	10	23	33	51	-13
West Brom	42	10	4	7	30	25	4	5	12	18	37	51	-14
Stoke	42	11	4	6	30	23	2	7	12	14	40	50	-19
Coventry	42	8	5	8	33	33	5	6	10	24	44	50	-20
Birmingham	42	7	7	7	19	18	5	5	11	20	32	48	-11
Notts County	42	6	7	8	31	36	4	4	13	19	36	41	-22
Wolves	42	4	8	9	15	28	2	3	16	12	52	29	-53

JUST UNBELIEVABLE: Why run when you can fly? The very special Andy Gray scores the first goal in the FA Cup win against Stoke City

The Match...

ANDY'S A HORIZONTAL HITMAN

STOKE CITY 0 EVERTON 2
FA Cup, third round, January 7, 1984

Stoke City (4-4-2): Fox, Bould, Hampton, James, Dyson, McAughtrie, Palmer, McIlroy (Maskery), O'Callaghan, Maguire, Chamberlain.
Everton (4-4-2): Southall, Stevens, Bailey, Ratcliffe, Mountfield, Reid, Irvine, Heath, Sharp, Gray, Sheedy. Sub: Richardson.
Referee: Mr. M. Peck (Kendall).
Goals: Gray (67), Irvine (84) 0-2.
Bookings: McIlroy (Stoke), Bailey and Stevens (Everton).
Conditions: Pitch cutting up, cold and windy.
Attendance: 16,482.

By Ken Rogers

EVERTON striker Andy Gray took to the air at Stoke on Saturday to launch the Blues towards the fourth round of the F.A. Cup.

The flying Scot became a magnificent horizontal hit man in the 67th minute of this highly competitive tie. He dived forward with tremendous agility to send a Kevin Sheedy cross looping into the net off the underside of the bar.

It was a header of the highest class, a superb exhibition of centre-forward play that brought a deafening salute from the giant army of Evertonians who had out-sung and out-shouted the home fans all afternoon.

And as if the sight of one flying Scot was not enough to demoralise troubled Stoke, the Blues produced another in the form of midfield man Alan Irvine.

He had been turning defender Peter Hampton inside out with his skill and pace, and the pay-off came in spectacular style six minutes from time.

Adrian Heath, putting in a gritty display against his old club, clipped a telling ball down the right flank that Irvine took in his stride.

He attacked the box, left Hampton for dead and drilled an unstoppable left-foot shot into the roof of the net to make it 2-0.

If Gray's was the decisive strike, Irvine's effort was the knockout punch that left Stoke with a real crisis on their hands.

The Potteries club are managerless after the sacking of Richie Barker, and the acting boss, Bill Asprey, still doesn't know where he stands in terms of a permanent job.

The threat of relegation is hanging over the Victoria Ground, with only Wolves between Stoke and the bottom rung.

Now the chance of a money-spinning cup run has disappeared. The misery of the home dressing room was written all over the face of Asprey as he attended the post-match press conference.

Yet it might have been so different if striker Brendan O'Callaghan could have matched the lethal heading ability of his opposite number Gray. The talented Mark Chamberlain, courted unsuccessfully by Sunderland recently, had dropped a pinpoint cross into the Everton box in the first half and O'Callaghan was perfectly placed to break the deadlock.

But he directed his solid header straight at goalkeeper Neville Southall, who was to make a couple of vital second half saves at the feet of the same player.

It was a typical cup-tie, with plenty of end-to-end action to keep the fans bubbling with excitement. The Blues were not prepared to sit back, and after 15 minutes Heath saw a goal-bound effort kicked clear by defender David McAughtrie after Graeme Sharp had headed on John Bailey's free kick.

The pitch was heavily sanded in places and cutting up badly. Peter Reid was ready to plough through the energy-sapping conditions in the vital early exchanges with a couple of long and threatening runs. Sharp was another who showed total commitment. He had been out for six games with an ankle injury, but returned to team up with Gray and run himself into the ground over the 90 minutes.

It's the only way cup-ties can be won and Everton had the resolve to produce the goods. Whenever Stoke tried to penetrate they found Kevin Ratcliffe in superb form in the Blues' defence.

Everton's attacking promise as the first half progressed saw Heath make space for himself before drilling into the side netting. Then Gray swivelled and hooked over after Graeme Sharp had set up the chance in the box.

Stoke had been banking on the skills of England man Chamberlain and the solid midfield play of Robbie James to inspire their fortunes. After 56 minutes it looked as though the home side would take the lead when a cutting through ball caught out the visitors' defence.

The luckless O'Callaghan only had Southall to beat, but the keeper spread himself to save with his legs. It was to prove a costly miss as Gray and Irvine took centre stage to claim the F.A. Cup glory with those two magnificent goals.

STAR MAN

Everton had a number of candidates for the man-of-the-match award. Goalkeeper Neville Southall made three excellent saves, while Kevin Ratcliffe was outstanding in defence.

But my verdict finally went to Alan Irvine, the man with the old-fashioned wing skills, who was always a threat on the flanks. He crushed Stoke's revival hopes with that superb late strike.

HOWARD KENDALL
– inside the dressing room

I was delighted when our FA Cup campaign began at Stoke in January, 1984. It took me back to one of my former clubs. What lives with me from that day is the sight of the army of Evertonians who travelled down to the Potteries. Of course, I was well aware of the passion of our fans, having revelled in that 1969/70 Championship winning year as a player before later captaining the club. I had a complete grasp of the difference they could make in any situation. At Stoke, I was thinking what to say in my team talk when I remembered that it was one of the few grounds with a window in the dressing room. I could hear the Evertonians singing and chanting. They were making a tremendous noise. I just opened the window as wide as possible and said: "Listen to that." I didn't need a rousing team talk. The fans did it for me.

Lots of things stick in your mind. I'll never forget Andy Gray that day. He was cup-tied in the Milk Cup and it seemed to make him doubly determined in the FA Cup, not that he ever needed much motivating. He was going round geeing everyone up. Out on the pitch, he got the first goal after about 67 minutes. It was a typical Gray effort. Andy would go for a header when other players would use their feet. He was a tremendous centre-forward, one of the old school in a way. There was a time when big battering ram number nines marauded up front in every game, men like Andy Lockhead of Burnley who, in my day, was one of the toughest strikers in the business.

Of course, Evertonians were brought up on the legend of the great centre-forward. We produced the greatest of them all, Dixie Dean, and had a long line of them down the years, people like Dave Hickson, Fred Pickering and Joe Royle.

Andy was in good company and he understood what it meant to Evertonians. He would dive in amongst the boots, as brave as they come. No wonder the fans loved him.

Our second goal against Stoke was scored by wide midfielder Alan Irvine, now Everton's assistant manager. Alan was a skilful young Scot who had been signed by my predecessor Gordon Lee shortly before he parted company with the Blues. I took Alan with us on tour to Japan and that was where he made his debut - against Inter Milan! Of course, another Everton midfielder had made his debut against the same club many years earlier in very different circumstances in the European Cup - Colin Harvey.

Alan's debut was less memorable. He was one of our substitutes and couldn't believe it when I told him he was going on. He was incredibly excited and immediately set off on a mazy run the first time he got the ball.

Unfortunately his legs were like jelly and he fell over. Alan had lots of skill and clearly had a good football brain because he has developed into a respected coach.

The Cup runs that year were a major bonus, but people sometimes forget that it was matched by our improvement in the league after such a poor start. Only Liverpool had a better league record after Christmas 1983. We lost just three out of 22 in the league.

IS IT IN? Andy Gray chips the keeper as he threatens once more against Notts County in the FA Cup sixth round, 1984

The Match...

ANDY GOES FLAT OUT FOR WEMBLEY

NOTTS COUNTY 1 EVERTON 2
FA Cup, Sixth Round, March 10, 1984

Notts County (4-4-2): Leonard, Lahtinen, Clarke, Richards, Kilcline, Hunt, O'Neill, Christie, McCulloch, McParland (Goodwin 58), Chiedozie.
Everton (4-4-2): Southall, Stevens, Bailey, Ratcliffe, Mountfield, Reid, Irvine, Richardson, Sharp, Gray, Sheedy (Harper 58).
Referee: Mr J. Martin (Alton, Hants).
Goals: Richardson (6 minutes) 0-1; Chiedozie (17 minutes) 1-1; Gray (47 minutes) 1-2.
Conditions: Heavy rain late in the game; pitch heavy.
Bookings: Mountfield and Richardson (Everton); Hunt (County).
Attendance: 19,534.

By Ken Rogers

EVERTON striker Andy Gray, ineligible for the Milk Cup Final against Liverpool, is determined to taste the glamour and excitement of Wembley on the FA Cup front. The Scottish star produced a remarkable matchwinner in Saturday's quarter-final at Notts County, a diving header that few strikers would have attempted, let alone steered into the back of the net.

The tie was balanced on a knife-edge at 1-1 when the Blues gained a free-kick after 47 minutes. Kevin Sheedy lofted the ball towards the box where it soared over the head of Graeme Sharp and his marker David Hunt.

Gray suddenly arrived from nowhere, launching himself along the wet and slippery surface to make a horizontal header. He made contact a matter of inches above the ground and goalkeeper Mike Leonard had no chance as the ball edged inside the right hand post.

Everton's magnificent travelling army of 10,000 fans roared their delight as Gray took off on a triumphant run before being mobbed by his team-mates.

Those supporters were to inspire the players every inch of the way as the Blues shook off County's determined efforts to get back into the game.

Whenever the home side did penetrate they found goalkeeper Neville Southall in brilliant form in the Everton goal.

It finally drained the Nottingham side's spirit and in the closing stages it was Howard Kendall's men who were looking stronger, with both Gray and Sharp going desperately close to increasing the lead.

Everton thoroughly deserved victory, although the edited Match of the Day highlights possibly did not reflect the true measure of their performance.

County were certainly a lively proposition in the first half, threatening mainly from corners and free-kicks. But it was Everton who made a flying start, taking the lead after six minutes through Kevin Richardson.

The midfield man, out recently with a fractured wrist, played 75 minutes of reserve football on Friday night.

Kendall thrust him straight into this game in place of the injured Adrian Heath. Richardson was still wearing a protective covering on his arm as a precaution.

When Gary Stevens launched a long throw-in towards the County area the imposing presence of Gray forced two defenders to miss the ball completely.

Richardson nipped in quickly to head home from close range and the stage was set for a thrilling clash

The home side showed real character to get back on terms after 17 minutes.

Southall had made an unbelievable save from Ian McCulloch's goal-bound header, but the skilful John Chiedozie latched onto the rebound to make it 1-1.

It was end-to-end stuff, Everton pulling together a sweeping six-

man move that ended with goalkeeper Leonard denying Sharp with an instinctive save.

Up at the other end Southall tipped over the top as Finnish star Aki Lahtinen curled in a shot with the outside of his right boot. The keeper then saved brilliantly from McCulloch.

The game was wide open until that Gray special put the Blues back in the driving seat.

With the rain sweeping down and sapping the energy of both teams, Everton finished with a flourish. Gray moved in on the box, only for the advancing Leonard to deflect his shot off target.

Then Kilcline kicked off the line as an effort from Sharp rolled to a halt in the mud.

Over two minutes of extra time delayed the Blues' victory march, but referee Martin finally signalled an end.

One Wembley date is assured on March 25th and another is now just 90 minutes away, exciting times for fans who are enjoying every minute of this revival and playing their part along the way.

 **STAR MAN**

Everton's confidence and fighting spirit threw up a number of candidates for the man-of-the-match award. Neville Southall was superb in goal and Peter Reid demonstrated once again that he is in great form in midfield. But the vote goes to Andy Gray. Few strikers would have produced that match winner and his all-round performance emphasised his quality as a class centre-forward.

HOWARD KENDALL
– inside the dressing room

The Notts County game will be forever remembered for that sensational diving header, scored by Andy Gray. I also remember it for another reason. Kevin Richardson had his arm in plaster at that time. A referee had refused to allow him to play in a reserve game during his comeback because he claimed the heavy plaster was too dangerous, not for Kevin but for anyone he might catch with it. As soon as we got to Notts County I took our midfielder into the referee's room. I explained that another official had deemed the plaster dangerous and that we had listened carefully and replaced it with a lighter cast. The ref just said: "Okay, that's fine."

It was the same plaster! What can I say? Refs miss enough things on the pitch. I didn't mind him missing this one off it! Kevin was important to us and played his part in a great away win to help us reach the semi-final, including scoring the first goal.

It was one of those days when we needed to be mentally tough because of the conditions and the ground. When top teams go to a venue like that and one of the ends is devoid of atmosphere, it tends not to motivate them. I think the goal-end where Andy scored had very little on it except the dressing rooms.

But Andy, for one, had built himself up for that day. He desperately wanted to go to the FA Cup Final because he was ineligible in the Milk Cup. People always talk about that diving header. I remember saying in the press conference that he "rotivated the ground with his nose" as he dived in. Possibly, at that time, he was not capable of moving his feet quick enough to get there and slide the ball home. But he had the ambition and the determination to get there.

Some strikers might have just left it and indicated with their body language that it was not a clear chance with the ball too far away. Not Andy. He made it into a goalscoring moment. Maybe another player might have been sharp enough to try to get a foot to the ball, but again, Andy was different.

In terms of being single-minded, he just said to himself: "That ball is mine". He launched himself forward on his stomach, aware that he would slide forward at pace on the greasy surface.

When you think about it, Duncan Ferguson has been one of those who can tower above people to win headers and score goals. I don't think Andy towered above people, although the name Steve Sherwood immediately shouts in your face! He could leap and he had great timing, but many of his headed goals were executed low down. I recall goals against Sunderland and Fortuna Sittard.

He would put in a header when others would try a volley. I remember going to an event at Anfield for Bob Paisley at the time I signed Andy. There were a few sniggers in the room. I could sense it. They were saying to themselves: "What's going on over there?" because of the doubts about the player's long-term fitness. They soon found out what was going on. We were building a great side of which Andy was a key part for two memorable years.

ANDY TACTICS: The only way to stop Gray. Climb all over him. Action from the April, 1984 clash against Southampton at the Dell

The Match...

HEATH'S EXTRA SPECIAL STRIKE CLINCHES BLUES' WEMBLEY DOUBLE

EVERTON 1 SOUTHAMPTON 0
FA Cup, Semi-Final, April 14, 1984

Everton (4-4-2): Southall, Stevens, Bailey, Ratcliffe, Mountfield, Reid, Curran, Heath, Gray, Steven (Sharp 105 minutes), Richardson.
Southampton (4-4-2): Shilton, Mills, Dennis, Williams, Agboola, Wright, Holmes, Moran, Worthington, Armstrong, Wallace. Sub: Puckett.
Referee: Mr. G. Courtney (County Durham).
Conditions: Bright sunshine, pitch patchy.
Goal: Heath (117 minutes) 1-0.
Bookings: Ratcliffe (Everton), Wallace (Southampton).
Attendance: 46,587.

By Ken Rogers

ARIAN HEATH, a player whose goals have been pure gold to Everton this season, struck it rich again on Saturday, with an F.A. Cup semi-final winner that completely shattered rivals Southampton.

The tie, goalless at 90 minutes, drifted into an energy-sapping spell of extra time at Highbury in which the Blues had the commitment and strength to clinch their second Wembley appearance of the season. The man of the moment - not for the first time in cup action - was the diminutive Heath.

He has developed a happy knack of producing vital goals from both midfield and attack.

Who could forget his second half equaliser against Coventry in the Milk Cup that was the real turning point for Everton's season?

A late strike against Oxford in the same competition was to deny the Third Division outfit a shock giant-killing victory and keep a run bubbling that was to end in the historic all-Merseyside final against Liverpool. But Heath rated Saturday's crucial effort against Southampton, scored three minutes from the end of extra time, as the most satisfying of his whole career. If anyone was going to break the deadlock for the Blues in this clash, it was going to be the lively No. 8.

Manager Howard Kendall had left out Graeme Sharp and pushed Heath up front, alongside Andy Gray. It was hoped that his pace and energy would prove decisive against Southampton's sweeper system and it almost paid off in the opening minutes, when a careless throw-in by Mark Dennis saw Heath threaten to the right of the box. It took a vital challenge from Mark Wright to clear the danger. In the closing stages of normal time, Heath went desperately close to opening the scoring. His speed took him clear of the Saints' back four, but he pulled his shot wide with only Peter Shilton to beat.

Minutes later, Heath cashed in on determined work by Peter Reid and Terry Curran to finally get the ball past the England keeper, but up popped the experienced Mick Mills to clear off the line.

Heath was forced to wait for his moment of glory. His contribution had been matched by Southampton's Danny Wallace, a major threat to the Blues' Wembley dreams. Operating down both flanks, he carved out a number of chances. Wallace would be forced to join the Neville Southall Appreciation Society. He watched in awe as the Welsh international keeper turned a shot from the edge of the box round the post for a corner.

The little Saints' forward thought he had found a way through straight after half time, but Southall was equal to the confrontation once again.

Terry Curran, the man who sent Southampton to Wembley in 1979 with a League Cup matchwinner against Leeds, found it extremely difficult to make an impression against his old club. With no natural left-sided player, the Blues were looking to Curran to impose himself on the other flank.

It was only in the later stages of an evenly contested game that he finally began to threaten the Saints, with Everton looking the

stronger of the two teams in extra time.

The energy seemed to drain from the legs of the South coast players and defender Mark Wright later made a remarkable outburst that his skipper, Steve Williams, was not fully fit and should never have played. He was overshadowed by the running and strength of Peter Reid who signalled Everton's intentions at the start of the extra period with a solid shot that was held by Shilton.

Mountfield came forward to head over the top and Gray, in typical style, went sliding in on his stomach in a desperate bid to reach a right-wing cross.

The Scottish striker then cursed himself for a disappointing miss from eight yards, failing to connect cleanly and giving the Saints a temporary reprieve.

The Blues brought on Graeme Sharp in place of Trevor Steven, who had worked extremely hard in normal time. With 116 minutes on the clock, Heath popped up to floor Southampton with his 15th goal of the season.

The fans exploded into song... Howie's Army, we're heading to Wembley.

★ STAR MAN

Everton had excellent candidates for their man-of-the-match award. Neville Southall made a couple of magnificent saves to deny the Saints, while Peter Reid was a solid figure in the centre of midfield.

But the verdict went to Adrian Heath, a man whose goal contribution in 1984 has transformed Everton's season. His return has been matched by his enthusiasm and determination. The little striker is developing into a real match winner.

HOWARD KENDALL
– inside the dressing room

I had a very difficult selection decision to make before the FA Cup semi-final against Southampton at Highbury. I finally decided to leave Graeme Sharp out. There is never a good time to tell a player, especially when a game is so important. I broke the news to Graeme on the day during our morning walk. He wasn't happy. Almost certainly he was thinking beyond the semi itself. If we got through, would he also be a bystander in the Final? Of course, Graeme would ultimately be a Wembley goal hero, but I opted for Andy Gray and Adrian Heath up front against the Saints and Inchy scored a famous winner.

As a manager and a coach, there was some satisfaction after the game because a little bit of homework contributed to the victory. We watched them in the lead-up to the semi. It was clear that they were vulnerable at set-pieces. Frank Worthington was up front for them, a skilful and talented forward but not the most disciplined.

He always went back to help defend at set-pieces and I thought that if Derek Mountfield jogged up with him, instinctively forcing the striker to mark our big defender, then it might pay off. Derek could always score goals in these situations, or play a part.

As it turned out, he got a touch on the cross that led to the goal that Inchy buried at the far post. All Evertonians still love to see the picture of him wheeling away with that beaming smile on his face. On the bench, we just smiled because there was more than a little bit of satisfaction that information we had passed on had paid off so handsomely.

For me, winning the semi-final was almost as good as winning the Cup itself. The game against Southampton was in London at Highbury. We got the train back home after the Wembley FA Cup win, but we had the team bus with us for the semi.

I will never forget the motorway, packed full of Evertonians who were all waving and chanting as they passed us. They could see all the lads, not like it is now with blacked out windows on the coaches. We were passing no one because I told the driver to take his foot off the gas and take as long as he liked to get us back. We had a lot of celebrating to do. It was the start of something special. We were back at Wembley for the second time in a matter of months and determined that this time we would end up with a trophy in our hands.

I had been the youngest player of the century to appear in a final in 1964 when I turned out for Preston 20 days before my 18th birthday. We were the Second Division underdogs and so when we lost to West Ham I was not as devastated as I might have been. It was different in 1968 when, as an Everton player, I was in a top class side that lost to West Brom. That result was a massive blow.

As we headed home from Highbury, I could revel in another impending FA Cup Final challenge, this time as a manager. I was thrilled that our army of fans were proud again and that we were good enough to take the next step.

WEMBLEY HERE WE COME!: The Blues squad all present and correct

The Match...

I GUESS THAT'S WHY THEY CALL IT THE BLUES!

EVERTON 2 WATFORD 0
FA Cup Final, May 19, 1984

Everton (4-4-2): Southall, Stevens, Bailey, Ratcliffe, Mountfield, Reid, Steven, Heath, Richardson, Sharp, Gray, Sub: Harper.
Watford (4-2-4): Sherwood, Bardsley, Price (Atkinson 58), Taylor, Perry, Sinnott, Callaghan, Johnston, Reilly, Jackett, Barnes.
Referee: Mr. J. Hunting (Leicestershire).
Goals: Sharp (38) 1-0. Gray (51) 2-0.
Conditions: Warm and bright afternoon, turning cloudy.
Attendance: 100,000.
Receipts: £915,000.

By Ken Rogers

WHAT a day, what a season. Merseyside's Big Two stand supreme, the untouchables of English soccer. The League Championship, the Milk Cup, the FA Youth Cup and now the FA Cup itself all reside within the city. Liverpool can still add European glory to this stunning array of silverware, but for the moment their famous rivals Everton are basking proudly in the spotlight, winners again after 14 long years.

Saturday's 2-0 victory over Watford saw Howard Kendall's blue and white army take Wembley by storm. It was an occasion to cherish; the friendly final when rival fans shared a laugh and a joke before the game, posed with each other for photographs and revelled in the atmosphere and excitement of a marvellous occasion.

But cup finals are all about winners and Everton's unshakable determination to claim that elusive piece of silverware was to prove decisive. Watford boss Graham Taylor had talked about enjoying the match and being part of a great day.

His rival Howard Kendall, a two-time Wembley loser, could only talk about winning. Goals from twin strikers Graeme Sharp and Andy Gray were to give the Blues' boss possibly his proudest ever moment, surpassing even his achievement in helping win the League Championship for Everton back in 1970.

The Ball-Harvey-Kendall midfield trio was to become legendary at Goodison. Now the Kendall and Colin Harvey backroom link has proved just as potent. They both choked back the tears as Kevin Ratcliffe held aloft the FA Cup. A season of swinging fortunes had ended on an unforgettable high note.

Even before a ball was kicked Everton knew that the biggest threat to their chances would come from the talented John Barnes. The young winger was to live up to his exciting reputation, shaking the Blues early in the game with his pace, strength and superb skill.

It's a pleasure to watch Barnes in full flight, a player who can light up any match with his natural ability. The task of containing him fell to another impressive young player, Blues' right back Gary Stevens.

He was to rise to the challenge magnificently and as Everton imposed themselves on their opponents, the fans were to salute the adventure of another bright talent - Trevor Steven. What a game he was to have, finally laying on the cross from the right that saw Gray kill off Watford with typical spring and strength after 51 minutes.

From that point there could only be one result with Everton firmly in the driving seat and their opponents struggling to pick themselves up off the floor.

Yet what a start Taylor's side had made. Lee Sinnott was using his ability as a long throw specialist to good effect, aiming for the giant George Reilly. In the first minute a knock on gave Barnes a

close range heading chance with Neville Southall making a fine save.

Everton's response was a dangerous cross from Steven that was glanced wide by Sharp and a strong run and shot into the side netting from Kevin Richardson.

It was an outstanding first half, Adrian Heath setting off on a twisting chase for goal before attempting a chipped shot that was deflected for a corner.

Watford bounced back, the Barnes magic flickering as his body swerve took him away from both Gary Stevens and Derek Mountfield. He got in his shot on the edge of the box with Southall spreading himself, but it was Mountfield who recovered to block the effort.

The pressure wasn't over for the Blues with Les Taylor arriving to hammer inches wide of the left hand post. Both sides had created good opportunities and Peter Reid, Everton's Player of the Year with 11 man-of-the-match nominations in the Echo during the season, showed his strength to shake off Kenny Jackett before curling a tremendous effort wide of the upright.

The momentum of the game and the vast number of scoring chances at both ends made this an intriguing and entertaining final. Everton began slowly, then stepped up a gear to live up to their billing as favourites.

The decisive blow came after 38 minutes. Wembley erupted in a sea of blue and white as Sharp suddenly found himself with the space just inside the box to strike a brilliant opener.

Gary Stevens had won a challenge with Barnes, the ball breaking forward for Sharp to control and lash his shot into the corner of the net with goalkeeper Steve Sherwood completely helpless. The fans roared their delight. Watford were forced to dig deep into their reserves of character and spirit, but six minutes into the second half it was effectively all over.

Trevor Steven's skill took him past full-back Neil Price. The midfield man sent over a teasing cross that looked ripe for the keeper to hold but Gray rose with power and suddenly the ball was in the back of the net.

Watford, pushed by Bob Wilson later on Match of the Day, complained that Sharp's effort was offside and that Gray had fouled Sherwood for the second. But to suggest that this victory was anything but fully deserved is an insult to a memorable match.

The headlines in the Echo's Wembley souvenir edition, sported in many cars on the motorway, had already said it all for the Evertonians: WE'RE BACK.

STAR MAN

In weighing up the contenders for the Everton man-of-the-match you have to look at the battling efforts of goal heroes Graeme Sharp and Andy Gray, the undoubted ability of goalkeeper Neville Southall and the midfield determination of Peter Reid and Kevin Richardson.

But no one would deny that two young players on the right flank played a key role in this triumph. Full-back Gary Stevens fought a mighty battle with John Barnes, a performance that was to earn him a salute from England boss Bobby Robson. The vote was finally edged to Trevor Steven, whose adventure and skill caused Watford all kinds of problems and who is emerging as one of the most exciting prospects in the game.

HOWARD KENDALL
– inside the dressing room

League games against Watford had proved high scoring affairs, probably because of the style of play Graham Taylor adopted. He was a disciple of the long-ball tactics and it clearly worked for them. They missed out the midfield and launched things forward although it should be remembered that they were not devoid of skill at that time. A young John Barnes was one of their key players. When we played them at Vicarage Road in the February of '84, the game finished 4-4. I felt we could always score against them and knew that if we could get the ball down and play at Wembley then we would win the Cup.

There was another key difference between us. Because success at this level was new to them, they felt that just being at Wembley was a great day out and a source of real pride. For us, it was all about winning. I didn't just see it as a trophy and a launching pad to further things, but an opportunity to test ourselves in Europe. Graeme Sharp's disappointment at missing the semi had him fired up and I also selected both Adrian Heath and Andy Gray. As it turned out Sharp and Gray were our goal heroes on a day none of us will ever forget.

Of course, Andy's goal has earned some notoriety. Watford goalkeeper Steve Sherwood still claims he was fouled when Andy jumped in for that header. I have watched the video many times. It could have gone either way. A modern ref would have disallowed it because they don't like any contact. But when Andy turned away in animated celebration with the ball in the back of the net, there was no way the ref was going to blow for a foul. I don't think there was deliberate contact or an elbow on Sherwood. Andy just climbed for it in the way centre-forwards do. He was totally committed and maybe Sherwood wasn't. Possibly the keeper was looking at Andy rather than the ball.

We had been given an early warning when Les Taylor had a 25-yard effort deflected just wide by John Bailey. That focused us even more and after Graeme's opener crashed into the bottom corner, we were never going to lose.

The reception we got back on Merseyside was something I will never forget. Later, I would take the FA Cup home for some personal photos. Let's put it this way. It was the nicest thing I've ever slept with! Beautiful!

1983/84 FA CUP STATS

Home in bold (semi-final and final neutral).

ROUND	DATE	TEAM	RESULT
3	Jan 6	Stoke City	W 2-0 Gray, Irvine
4	**Jan 28**	**Gillingham**	**D 0-0**
R	Jan 31	Gillingham	D 0-0
R	Feb 6	Gillingham	W 3-0 Sheedy 2, Heath
5	**Feb 18**	**Shrewsbury**	**W 3-0 Irvine Reid, Griffin o.g.**
6	Mar 10	Notts County	W 2-1 Gray, Richardson
SF*	Apr 14	Southampton	W 1-0 Heath
F+	May 19	Watford	W 2-0 Sharp, Gray.

*Played at Highbury
+ Played at Wembley

1983/84 LEAGUE STATS:

Home games in bold.

AUG			
27	**Stoke**	W 1-0 Sharp	22,658
29	West Ham	L 0-1	20,375

SEP			
3	Coventry	D 1-1 Sheedy	12,532
6	Ipswich Town	L 0-3	16,543
10	**West Brom**	D 0-0	15,548
17	Tottenham	W 21-1 Reid, Sheedy	29,125
24	**Birmingham**	D 1-1 Sharp (pen)	15,253

OCT			
1	Notts County	W 1-0 Reid	7,949
15	**Luton Town**	L 0-1	14,325
22	Watford	W 1-0 Johnson	13,571
29	Leicester	L 0-2	10,953

NOV			
6	Liverpool	L 0-3	40,875
12	**Nottm Forest**	W 1-0 Heath	17,546
19	Arsenal	L 1-2 King (pen)	24,330
26	**Norwich**	L 0-2	14,106

DEC			
3	Man Utd	W 1-0 Sheedy	43,664
10	**Aston Villa**	D 1-1 Gray	15,810
17	QPR	L 0-2	11,608
26	**Sunderland**	D 0-0	18,683
27	Wolves	L 0-3	12,761
31	**Coventry**	D 0-0	13,659

JAN			
2	Birmingham	W 2-0 King, Stevens	10,004
14	Stoke	D 1-1	7,945
21	**Tottenham**	W 2-1 Heath 2	18,003

FEB			
4	**Notts County**	W 4-1 Heath 3, Sheedy(pen)	13,016
11	West Brom	D 1-1 Mountfield	10,313
25	Watford	D 4-4 Sharp 2, Gray, Heath	16,982

MAR			
3	**Liverpool**	D 1-1 Harper	51,245
13	Nottm Forest	L 0-1	13,647
17	**Ipswich Town**	W 1-0 Mountfield	18,013
20	Leicester	D 1-1 Richardson	15,142
31	Southampton	W 1-0 Gray	20,244

APRIL			
7	Luton Town	W 3-0 Heath 2, Mountfield	9,224
9	**Arsenal**	D 0-0	21,174
17	Southampton	L 1-3 Richardson	16,978
21	Sunderland	L 1-2 Heath	15,876
23	**Wolves**	W 2-0 Gray, Steven	17,185
28	Norwich	D 1-1 Gray	13,624

MAY			
5	**Man Utd**	D 1-1 Wakenshaw	28,817
7	Aston Villa	W 2-0 Richardson, Sharp	16,792
12	**QPR**	W 3-1 Sharp 2, Heath.	20,679
14	West Ham	W 1-0 Richardson	25,452

Final League position: 7th in First Division.

WHERE DID YOU GET THAT HAT?: John Bailey in jubilant mood as the FA Cup is paraded at Wembley in 1984. Clockwise: Derek Mountfield, Bailey, Peter Reid, Kevin Ratcliffe, Alan Harper, Andy Gray, Gary Stevens, Adrian Heath, Graeme Sharp, Neville Southall, Kevin Richardson and Trevor Steven

TAKE THAT: (left) Graeme Sharp was simply unstoppable when he was in full flight for goal. He is pictured here in action against Birmingham City's Tony Coton in September, 1983

NICE ONE DEREK: For once big Nev needs a helping hand as Mountfield clears in front of goal in the 2-0 win at Villa Park in May, 1984

GOODISON GLORY: Adrian Heath (left) scores as part of a hat-trick in a 4-1 win over Notts County in February, 1984

ONE ON ONE: There was only ever going to be one winner as another goalkeeper falls victim to the predatory instincts of Graeme Sharp. Here he scores in a 3-1 win over Queens Park Rangers in May, 1984, the last home league game before the FA Cup Final

SNOW HERO: Andy Gray holds off a Stoke defender at the Victoria Ground in January, 1984

THANKS VERY MUCH: Kevin Ratcliffe collects the 1984 FA Cup from Princess Michael of Kent

GO-GO RICHO: Time to celebrate as the players rush in to congratulate a delighted Kevin Richardson after he scored in a 2-0 win at Villa in May, 1984

SLIDING IN: A Stoke City defender puts his foot in, but Adrian Heath has slipped the ball past him en route for goal in January, 1984

TRUSTY LEFT FOOT: Kevin Sheedy scores from the spot in a 4-1 win over Notts County in February, 1984

FLATTENED: Andy Gray (right) takes a tumble in the same game

SHOOTING POWER:
Andy Gray drives in a
shot against Stoke City
in January, 1984

WATCHING THE LINE: Graeme Sharp threatens Stoke City in January, 1984

HANDY ANDY: Gray leaps high to out jump David O'Leary in a clash with Arsenal at Highbury

HANDS UP FOR GLORY: Has there ever been a better goalscoring centre-half than Derek Mountfield? Here he celebrates after scoring his first ever goal at Goodison, plundered in the 1-0 win over Ipswich Town in March, 1984. Terry Butcher is the despairing Ipswich defender

SIMPLY UNSTOPPABLE: Two defenders but only ONE Andy Gray, scoring at Norwich in April, 1984

SO CLOSE:
Graeme Sharp watches the ball fly just wide against Spurs in a 2-1 home win in April, 1984

YES, HE COULD HEAD AS WELL!: Kevin Sheedy shows there was more to his armoury than a lethal left foot against Stoke in January, 1984

PERFECT POISE: Trevor Steven drives in a superb right foot shot against Southampton in March, 1984

LOVE IS . . .
Another goal celebration as the boys in Blue show the togetherness that summed up the Eighties. This elation followed a last minute equaliser in a remarkable 4-4 draw against Watford in February, 1984

LEAP OF FAITH:
The totally committed Derek Mountfield is surrounded by a posse of Wolves defenders as the Blues try to battle back against Wolves in December, 1983

SPURRED ON: Adrian Heath scores one of two goals against Tottenham in January, 1984

WATCH OUT, DEREK'S ABOUT: Mountfield's first ever goal for Everton, scored at West Brom in February, 1984

SHOUT GRAY FOR GLORY: The wide smile of Andy Gray lights up Goodison, with a little help from Alan Irvine

I'M GUNNING FOR YOU: The sheer determination of Peter Reid is captured here against Arsenal at Highbury in November, 1983

GOAL HERO: Adran Heath (hidden) scores a crucial Milk Cup goal against Coventry in November, 1983

TOTAL FOCUS: Graeme Sharp keeps Mark Lawrenson on his toes in the March, 1984, Mersey derby (left)

RATS THE BOY: Kevin Ratcliffe goes forward to put Birmingham under pressure (far left) in September, 1983

BY THE LEFT:
Graeme Sharp hammers
home the matchwinner
on the opening day of the
1983/84 season at home
to Stoke City

SHEEDY, SHEEDY . . .
The elation of another great goal (left) as Graeme Sharp and Adrian Heath join Kevin's celebration after the midfielder scored the second goal in a 2-0 Milk Cup win over West Ham in December, 1983

WHERE'S THE KEEPER?: Who cares? As Mark Higgins watches Andy King's goal hit the back of the net (right) in the Milk Cup clash with West Ham. King is out of the picture

84/85 Howard's Way

IN THE SUMMER OF 1984 THE F.A. CUP WAS SITTING PROUDLY IN THE GOODISON PARK TROPHY ROOM FOLLOWING EVERTON'S POWERFUL WEMBLEY VICTORY OVER WATFORD.
THIS WAS THE CUP OF DREAMS, THE PIECE OF SILVERWARE THAT DIXIE HAD HELD ABOVE HIS HEAD IN 1933. THIS WAS FOOTBALL'S HOLY GRAIL, CARRYING THE FINGERPRINTS OF GORDON WEST, TOMMY WRIGHT, RAY WILSON, JIMMY GABRIEL, BRIAN LABONE, BRIAN HARRIS, ALEX SCOTT, MIKE TREBILCOCK, ALEX YOUNG, COLIN HARVEY AND DEREK TEMPLE . . . THE LEGENDARY CLASS OF '66
BUT AS THE FANS LOOKED AT THE FA CUP IN 1984, IT WAS ALL ABOUT HOWARD'S HEROES . . .

THE 1984/85 season would be all about building on a dream. Evertonians had waited a long time for their team to get back on top of the pile. Progress to the Milk Cup Final in March '84 had been the springboard to a second appearance under the famous Twin Towers and this time the ribbons on the Cup would definitely be royal blue. I have an image imprinted in my mind relating to the moment Kevin Ratcliffe thrust the FA Cup high into the air.

I was covering the game for the Liverpool Echo, but I didn't witness this moment of Everton history because the Wembley Press

Box was slung high under the stadium roof directly above the Royal Box. There was a highly frustrating moment when the players, climbing those steps to football heaven, disappeared from sight, only to reappear on the way back down.

All I could do was fix my gaze on manager Howard Kendall who was standing down on the pitchside track. In turn, his gaze was locked on skipper Ratcliffe as the Welsh international made his ascent into history in the footsteps of Dixie, Labby and the rest. Suddenly a broad smile spread across Howard's face. I knew Kevin had the Cup.

I will never forget the manager's expression and his sheer delight. He would tell me later that in those few precious seconds he knew that here was a piece of Everton history that no one could take away from him. He could carry the memory with him forever. But Kendall had no intention of the story ending there. He knew that winning the FA Cup was a wonderful achievement, but it wasn't a signal that Everton were the best. That accolade would only come when the club ran the marathon that was the Championship race and finished out in front.

Kendall, having finished eighth and then seventh twice, now plotted the ultimate coup. Everton would need a major leap forward to claim the number one slot, but he had seen enough during the two cup runs to convince him that the real glory game was now within his grasp.

The manager set about further strengthening his side for the start of the 1984/85 season. He signed Paul Bracewell from Sunderland for £250,000 in time for the talented midfielder to make his debut at Wembley as the Blues faced Liverpool in the Charity Shield. The Mersey Reds had not only won the league the previous year, but snatched the Milk Cup from Everton's grasp in a replay at Maine Road. The time had not just come for revenge

on that score, but to lay down a confident marker that the men from Goodison Park could match their arch-rivals in every way. Bracewell played his part in a 1-0 victory and the symbolism of that success was not lost on the Evertonians who travelled to London.

Kendall's vision in linking Bracewell's running and determination with Peter Reid's true grit, timing and supreme confidence would prove a masterstroke, although the fans were given a stark reality check when the Blues began the new league campaign with a 4-1 home reversal against Tottenham.

Was this really the start of Howard Kendall's brave new world? There were further doubts when Everton lost at West Brom, but six unbeaten matches after that was much more like it for the Cup holders, although a 5-4 Vicarage Road success over Wembley rivals Watford was possibly taking open attacking football a little bit too far. At key moments, managers have to make tough decisions. Boss Kendall, not for the first time in his managerial career, would act decisively to replace a great fans' favourite with some fresh legs. John Bailey had been highly influential in the FA Cup Final success, as well as winning our hearts and minds as the original Clown Prince of Wembley. Who could ever forget Bails' top hat and his giant "Elton" glasses during the lap of honour. The new man rarely seemed to smile, but he could play. Pat Van den Hauwe's arrival from Birmingham was another important step forward. 'Psycho Pat' lived up to his nickname and rivals genuinely began to fear the side that would play you off the park if you confronted them with a football challenge or meet you head on if you tried to mix it.

Defeat at Arsenal kept everyone's feet on the ground, but six straight victories after that set the pulses racing. This run included one of Graeme Sharp's finest moments when his now legendary bolt from the blue soared over Bruce Grobbelaar's head at Anfield to secure another Everton win over the old enemy. Manchester United were on the end of a real five star display and three goals ripped into the back of the Leicester net in a spell that left Kendall's men proudly looking down on the rest from the top of the table.

Norwich, of all teams, broke the run at Carrow Road and Chelsea would win 4-3 at Goodison, but the pace, power and supreme confidence of the Blues throughout this landmark season was a joy to behold.

Big Nev was ever-present between the posts on his way to becoming the football writers' Footballer of the Year. Gary Stevens showed pace and mobility from the right-back position. Derek Mountfield was the solid centre-half with the goal sense of a centre-forward. Kevin Ratcliffe was a real leader, on and off the pitch. A young man on the right was not dubbed "Tricky Trev" for nothing. PFA Player of the Year Reid and his partner Bracewell were the untouchables in the centre of the park and when Kevin Sheedy swung that lethal left boot, goalkeepers visibly trembled. Inchy and Sharpy were potent attacking partners early on before Cup hero Andy Gray got in his stride to terrorise opposing defences. The versatile Alan Harper was always ready to answer any challenge and Paul Wilkinson signed in late on to help clinch the double over Liverpool, by which time the title was in the bag.

The clincher came against Queens Park Rangers at Goodison Park on May 6, 1985 when Mountfield and Sharp scored the goals that captured Everton's eighth Championship triumph.

But this year had so much more to offer, not least a sensational European Cup Winners Cup Final success in Rotterdam over Rapid Vienna, preceded in the semis by the legend of Bayern Munich. Both of these games are featured in the selected match-

es that follow. The treble was but just a whisker away. Norman Whiteside's lone FA Cup Final winner for Manchester United put paid to that dream, but 1985 will live forever in the hearts and minds of the Goodison faithful. The Mersey Blues were truly back.

PROUD SKIPPER: Kevin Ratcliffe exchanges pennants with his Rapid Vienna counterpart Hans Kranklbefore the 1985 Cup Winners Cup Final

SAVE OF THE GAME: Bruce Grobbelaar goes full stretch to tip away this Gary Stevens' free-kick

The Match...

BOLT FROM THE BLUE!

LIVERPOOL 0 EVERTON 1
League, October 20, 1984

Liverpool (4-4-2): Grobbelaar, Neal, Lawrenson, Hansen, A. Kennedy, Wark, Molby, Whelan, Dalglish, Rush, Robinson. Sub: Lee.
Everton (4-4-2): Southall, Stevens, Mountfield, Ratcliffe, Van den Hauwe, Harper, Reid, Bracewell, Steven, Heath, Sharp. Sub: Gray.
Goal: Sharp (46) 0-1.
Corners: Liverpool 8, Everton 7.
Referee: Mr. N. Midgeley (Salford).
Attendance: 45,545

By Ian Hargraves

WHAT a difference 12 short months can make in football. This time last year Liverpool were heading for a unique treble in League, Milk Cup and Europe, while Everton were fighting the threat of relegation with their manager Howard Kendall being quoted as favourite for the Great Sack Race.

On Saturday it was Liverpool's turn to struggle against opponents who seem to have finally banished the kingsize inferiority complex that has bedeviled their efforts over the last decade.

Inspired by their performance in the two-legged Milk Cup Final, and again in the Charity Shield when they discovered their neighbours really could be beaten, they played to the form that has taken them near the top of the table and looked a really good side.

Now, as the Champions concentrate on rebuilding another great team, it is Everton who must surely carry Merseyside's hopes in the League and who, for the moment at least, are the standard bearers for tomorrow.

In a blustery, hard-fought struggle, full of entertainment and outstandingly refereed by Salford's Neil Midgeley, Everton always had the edge.

They were much quicker, both in thought and execution, and their lively central trio of Adrian Heath, Peter Reid and Paul Bracewell were always a step ahead of their opposite numbers, whose lack of pace has proved such a problem this season.

Reid was outstanding. Although he did not have a spectacular game, he was always there beating John Wark and Jan Molby to the ball, feeding Heath or Sharp with swift, accurate passes, and generally tidying up in midfield.

Behind him Kevin Ratcliffe and Mountfield kept a firm grip, not only on the welcome if match-rusty figure of Ian Rush, but on the much livelier Kenny Dalglish, who could well have swung the match given better support.

Gary Stevens confirmed his steady development at right-back and he hit a shot from a free-kick that Bruce Grobbelaar did well to push round the post.

Yet in the end it was one superb strike, by that exciting centre-forward Graeme Sharp, that decided the game.

Other chances came and went at both ends, but the one that counted was a sharply dipping 30-yard volley from Sharp, who pounced on a long, bouncing upfield punt by Stevens, shooting before Mark Lawrenson could get in his usual stifling challenge.

Grobbelaar, who had what is best described as an exciting game, had no chance with this effort.

It is a long time since I have seen so many blue jerseys at Anfield, especially in the Kop.

Like most who have watched both clubs this season, they could sense that Everton's moment had finally arrived, and that they were about to claim their first league victory on the ground for 14 years, and only their third anywhere against Liverpool in 34 League and Cup games.

When Everton last won at Anfield, in the season of 1969/70, they went on to take the Championship, and it is at least possible that they could do the same this season.

Liverpool will doubtless come again, when Rush and Craig Johnston are match fit and they have solved their pressing midfield problems.

By coincidence, they were in much the same situation in 1969/70 when Bill Shankly rebuilt an ageing side after the Cup defeat at Watford.

Hopefully, they will do the same again, but for the moment the glory is Everton's and it is they who have cause for celebration. Long may they enjoy it; they have waited long enough.

 STAR MAN

Although Everton's two strikers, Adrian Heath and Graeme Sharp, both played well with Sharp getting the vital goal, the most outstanding Blues' player was arguably in midfield.

Peter Reid ran the centre of the pitch, giving a magnificent display of all-round football and he was the key figure in his side's success.

HOWARD KENDALL
– inside the dressing room

It's remarkable how things can turn completely in the world of football. Towards the end of October, 1983, pressure was mounting as we struggled for results. In the November we came through that Milk Cup test against Coventry with just 9,000 fans in Goodison Park. In the previous round leaflets had been handed out saying "Kendall and Carter Out."

Now, just a year on, we could look back on a famous Milk Cup Final clash with Liverpool and a memorable FA Cup victory over Watford. To emphasise our improvement, the club's form in the league was on the up and up and our fans were full of confidence as we visited Anfield in the October to seek revenge against the old enemy with the Milk Cup in their trophy room.

One goal would settle it and it remains an effort that Evertonians always talk about, lashed home from long range by Graeme Sharp. It was our first win at Anfield in 14 years and that helped to make it even more special. It gave us the revenge for the Hansen handball at Wembley, but more important than that was the fact that it highlighted once again that we could match and beat them. Liverpool had a great team at that time and won a host of trophies in the Eighties. It proves what a great team we had with Merseyside the centre of the football universe.

INCHES AWAY: Grobbelaar relieved after watching Adrian Heath's cross fly by

SLIPPING AND SLIDING: Graeme Sharp in the thick of it against Manchester United. That's goalkeeper Gary Bailey tackling like a big centre-half

The Match...

BLUES TITLE REVIVAL IN A SPIN

EVERTON 5 MANCHESTER UNITED 0
League, October 27, 1984

Everton (4-4-2): Southall, Stevens, Mountfield, Ratcliffe, Van den Hauwe, Steven, Reid, Bracewell, Sheedy (Gray 68), Heath, Sharp.
Manchester United (4-4-2): Bailey, Moran (Stapleton 26), McQueen, Hogg, Albiston, Moses, Strachan, Robson, Olsen, Hughes, Brazil.
Bookings: Strachan, Robson, Hogg (Manchester United); Ratcliffe (Everton).
Referee: Mr. G. Tyson (Sunderland).
Scorers: Sheedy 2 (4, 23), Heath (34), Stevens (80), Sharp (85).
Attendance: 40,769.

By Ian Hargraves

THAT magnificent old Evertonian Joe Mercer put Saturday's victory over Manchester United in its true context when he said: "It was the best performance by any Everton side I can remember."

Even allowing for the natural enthusiasm of the moment, he wasn't far wrong.

You have to go back to the playing days of Kendall and Harvey, whose coaching skills were behind this latest triumph, to recall anything comparable, and it certainly overshadowed the whole of the last decade.

Manchester United arrived at Goodison as Championship favourites, fairly stuffed with internationals and having only lost one match previously.

They were totally outclassed by opponents whose all-round speed and inventiveness made a mockery of United's title pretensions.

Now manager Ron Atkinson faces the immense task of rebuilding their shattered confidence in time to avoid a repeat when the adversaries meet again at Old Trafford on Tuesday night.

Only two things give him much cause for hope. In the first place

Everton may be without Kevin Sheedy, whose two-goal comeback after injury triggered off the rout; secondly United centre-back Kevin Moran will either have recovered from concussion or will have been replaced.

Moran collided with Sheedy as the latter was in the act of heading Everton's first goal after only four minutes, and thereafter played in a complete daze until he was replaced by Stapleton 22 minutes later.

He had every excuse for not knowing what was going on around him, but there were plenty of occasions when his colleagues looked even more bewildered.

Like one or two sides before them, including Liverpool, United simply could not match the Blues' astonishing speed to the ball, let alone the precision of their passing.

The scene was set in the opening seconds when United kicked off, but immediately lost possession as Graeme Sharp and Peter Reid homed in like guided missiles.

Derek Mountfield could have scored even before Sheedy did.

The Irish international got his second after only 23 minutes and Adrian Heath made it three soon after.

The only miracle was that United somehow survived further setbacks until the last ten minutes when Gary Stevens and Sharp gave the scoreline a more accurate appearance.

Sheedy's performance fully justified manager Kendall's decision to make changes in the team that had won so well in Bratislava.

Everton truly hit the heights as their rapturous reception confirmed.

Strictly speaking, there should not have been a nomination this week because it is unfair to pick out an individual from such a superb team performance.

However, as we must have one, the nomination goes to Kevin Sheedy, simply because his two opening goals sent Everton on their way and because he played at least as well as everyone else until forced to limp off with a groin strain.

HOWARD KENDALL
— inside the dressing room

Having won at Anfield, we were full of confidence and self-belief. A week later we entertained Manchester United whose manager Ron Atkinson had said in his book that they were going to sweep everything before them that season.

We put five past them at Goodison where we were right on our game from the first whistle. The quality of the goals was tremendous with Kevin Sheedy grabbing two, supported by Adrian Heath, Graeme Sharp and Gary Stevens. I remember reading the Echo the following day.

That old Evertonian Joe Mercer was quoted as saying that it was "the greatest Everton performance he had ever seen."

That filled me with pride and I knew that there might be something special for us by the end of the season.

People ask me about wins like that and assume that, as a manager, they give you the most satisfaction. It certainly puts a smile on your face, but I sometimes got a greater satisfaction in seeing my team assert themselves against a very different type of opposition.

For instance, when Wimbledon got into the top flight, they were very difficult opponents in that they would try and drag you into a battle as well as utilising a direct long-ball game. We had the quality to play the Dons off the park with pure football and that said a lot about our team at that time.

It might seem strange to some fans, but beating Wimbledon 3-0 at Goodison was as satisfying from a coach's perspective as putting five past United. When you have quality against quality and come out on top it's satisfying enough. But when you have quality versus a system and you hold sway, it's special because it's a victory for football!

Whenever we played United, I had respect for their midfielder Bryan Robson. It's well documented that he was the first player I tried to sign when I became Everton manager. He was at West Brom at the time and Ron Atkinson wouldn't sell. Of course, Big Ron was happy to see Albion part company when he took over at United.

It's nice when a manager knows his players and how much they can achieve in the game. It was significant that Ron went back to Albion for both Robson and Remi Moses, both outstanding signings for United. We were just too good for them that day. What would we do now for a 5-0 win over United?

IN FULL STRIDE: The supremely skilful Trevor Steven scores the second goal against Spurs after rounding goalkeeper Ray Clemence.

The Match...

BLUES SWITCH UP FIRE POWER IN CHARGE TO TITLE

TOTTENHAM HOTSPUR 1 EVERTON 2
League, April 3, 1985

Tottenham Hotspur (4-4-2): Clemence, Thomas, Roberts, Miller, Bowen, Crooks, Perryman, Hoddle, Ardiles, Galvin, Falco. Sub: Brook on for Crooks after 78 minutes.
Everton (4-4-2): Southall, Stevens, Mountfield, Ratcliffe, Van den Hauwe, Steven, Reid, Bracewell, Sheedy, Gray, Sharp. Sub: Harper on for Gray after 57 minutes.
Referee: Mr. David Letts (Hampshire).
Goals: Gray (Everton) 10 minutes 0-1; Steven (Everton) 61 minutes 0-2; Roberts (Spurs) 74 minutes 1-2.
Corners: Spurs 8, Everton 4.
Attendance: 48,108.

By Ian Hargraves

MANY years ago Dutch side Ajax introduced a new concept of total football that took Europe by storm. Effectively it meant that virtually everyone in the side was capable of coming forward and either scoring or creating goals, so that opponents were overwhelmed.

Last night at White Hart Lane, Everton demonstrated a new, if less sophisticated, version of their own. In a match that may later be seen to have decided the Championship, they outplayed Spurs by virtue of their ability to oppose every Tottenham player with at least two challengers and so deny him the chance to do anything with the ball.

As with Ajax, every single member of the team was constantly involved, and if that involvement was largely destructive well, that was the nature of the game.

With a gale blowing straight down the pitch and more than 48,000 fans so tightly packed that police spent much of the first half shepherding the overflow round the ground, this was no game for the faint-hearted.

Wisely, Everton played it tight from the start, abandoning their favourite close-passing style almost completely and using the

wind to put pressure on the Spurs' defence.

Within five minutes of the start a huge punch by Neville Southall had almost put Trevor Steven through, and in the tenth minute came the incident that turned the match.

Miller mis-headed another enormous Southall clearance under pressure from Graeme Sharp and managed to knock the ball sideways into the path of the oncoming Andy Gray, whose fierce shot left Clemence helpless. From that moment Spurs were always struggling.

Hoddle was rarely allowed to create space for Falco and Galvin. Crooks frequently found himself caught offside and Ardiles, surprisingly preferred to Hazard after only a fortnight's serious preparation, could only function in fits and starts.

Everton had no hesitation in funnelling the ball back to Southall whenever possible. I counted 37 passes back to him - 22 of them in the first half - and took virtually no chances of surrendering that precious lead.

Apart from one fierce shot by Hoddle that swerved wide across the face of goal, Spurs rarely threatened. Southall had to push a high back pass from Gary Stevens round the post, and save a hard, long shot from Thomas, but was far less worried than Clemence, who watched both Kevin Sheedy and Sharp miss reasonable chances.

After 57 minutes Gray limped off to be replaced by Alan Harper but Spurs' hopes of a revival were soon dashed as Trevor Steven snapped up a second goal.

Sharp found himself wide on the right and although young Bowen seemed to have the danger covered he lost control and saw Steven sweep past him and take the ball round Clemence before netting.

For a time it looked as though Everton would run riot, for Sharp, Steven and Sheedy all broke clear in quick succession, but to their credit Spurs fought back well and a spectacular 20-yard shot from Roberts opened up the game again 16 minutes from the end.

Everton withstood a tremendous battering and three minutes from time Southall pulled off an almost unbelievable reflex save from a point-blank header by Falco that had the Spurs' players tearing their hair in disbelief.

It is almost impossible to single out individuals in what was essentially a team performance. Southall made an unbelievable save from Falco to make victory certain, while both Gray and Steven scored invaluable goals, but in the end my vote goes to Kevin Ratcliffe. He set a real captain's example, always in the thick of the fray and appropriately takes the award on behalf of the team.

HOWARD KENDALL
– inside the dressing room

The Tottenham game was crucial to us as we headed into the Championship home straight. We had just picked up a great result at Southampton where Kevin Richardson had scored twice. I actually left him out at White Hart Lane and I can still hear his Geordie accent ringing in my ears: "What have I gotta do, man?"

I'd decided to play Kevin Sheedy who was fit again after injury. You have to make tough decisions like that in football. As it turned out, we won again and Sheeds played well. I recall that Trevor Steven also had a great game on the other flank. It was a result that demonstrated to the London press that we had what it takes to win the title. Tottenham themselves were very much in the hunt and had more home games left than us. People felt this gave them the edge. We knew that if we beat them it would be a major psychological boost.

There was another personal reason why I wanted to win. The game should have been played in the January but was postponed with the Pools Panel declaring it a home win for Tottenham, even though we were top of the league. No points lost, but something we noted!

This was almost certainly the night when Neville Southall clinched his "Footballer of the Year" award. He made a save from Mark Falco late on that was world class and kept us in front after Roberts had pulled one back. As I said, the influential London media were out in force and they have a great pull in the voting for this particular award. Neville almost certainly made their minds up with that one great save although he had been tremendous all season.

We were all thrilled for Nev, but you look back and wonder if it was a bit of a backhanded compliment? You've just won the title and people are saluting your goalkeeper, suggesting you were under pressure on more than one occasion and that he was a regular saviour. Neville was outstanding when he needed to be, of course, and that save from Falco summed up his individual brilliance. He was one of the best in the world at that time and I recall one stop that was even better than the one against Tottenham.

We were playing Sheffield Wednesday and Neville dived instinctively to cover a shot. The ball took a sharp deflection to go the other way, but he somehow managed to change direction himself to make the save. For a big man, he was very athletic. He certainly won over the London press at White Hart Lane.

ONE STEP AHEAD: Graeme Sharp gets in his shot ahead of a QPR defender in a May, 1984 league game

The Match...

NEV'S JOY - THEN TITLE ELATION

EVERTON 2 QUEENS PARK RANGERS 0
League, May 6, 1985

Everton (4-4-2): Southall, Stevens, Van den Hauwe, Ratcliffe, Mountfield, Reid, Steven, Sharp, Gray, Bracewell, Sheedy. Sub: Richardson.
Queens Park Rangers (4-4-2): Hucker, Chivers, Dawes, Waddock, Wicks, Fenwick, Robinson, Fillery, Bannister, James, Gregory (McDonald 80 minutes).
Referee: Mr. J. Hough (Macclesfield).
Goals: Mountfield (24), Sharp (82) 2-0.
Booking: Sharp (Everton).
Attendance: 50,514.

By Ken Rogers

THE royal blue dream machine powered on to glory yesterday as the League Championship trophy returned to Goodison Park for the first time in 15 years.

A goal apiece from Derek Mountfield and Graeme Sharp overshadowed Queens Park Rangers and clinched the points that left Everton unassailable leaders of the First Division with five games still to play.

The FA Cup Final and the European Cup Winners Cup Final are still to come, but this was the prize that Howard Kendall and his outstanding young side wanted most of all. It was a day for Evertonians to savour from start to finish and 50,000 of them packed into the ground to get the celebrations off to an early start.

The news had spread that goalkeeper Neville Southall was the new Footballer of the Year and when he appeared to do a radio interview on the pitch before kick-off with his team mate and nearest rival Peter Reid, the fans roared their delight . . . the shape of things to come.

The carnival atmosphere increased as manager Kendall emerged to receive his Manager of the Month award, just a dress rehearsal for the ultimate accolade, Manager of the Year, that is surely just around the corner.

It was a fairytale script and even the rain that had been pouring down disappeared as the players emerged from the dressing room with Goodison Park a cauldron of excitement and expectation.

It was as if Rangers had simply travelled from London as a supporting act to an all-star Everton cast, but any nagging fears that the champagne might have to go on ice disappeared as the Blues set about the job in hand with the relentless determination that has been their hallmark this season.

It took them just 24 minutes to break the deadlock, and who better to send the Gwladys Street fans into ecstasy than a player who used to stand behind that famous goal himself - Derek Mountfield.

Rangers were forced to concede a corner as Reid's skill and determination took him on a bold run into the box. Kevin Sheedy's left foot swerved in the cross, Andy Gray and Pat Van den Hauwe both got a touch and Mountfield hammered a shot into the back of the net, the ball striking the underside of the bar and the keeper on the way in.

It was his 12th goal of the season, a record that many strikers would be proud of, let alone centre-halves. It eased the pressure and the tension and Everton suddenly had Rangers on the rack.

Graeme Sharp sent a bullet header towards the roof of the net that was tipped over by Peter Hucker. Then Reid shot narrowly wide and Sharp struck the right hand post after Sheedy had found him with a neat free kick.

Sharp was to have an eventful afternoon and he was booked after an incident with Gary Waddock. But the only thing on the Scottish striker's mind was the goal that would not only clinch

the Championship, but also take his personal haul to 30.

When it came, after 82 minutes, it was an effort that all of the great Everton centre-forwards of yesteryear would have been proud of.

Paul Bracewell linked with Van den Hauwe, the cross from the left was perfect and there was Sharp, rising majestically like some latter-day Dixie Dean, Tommy Lawton, or Joe Royle to power a header into the roof of the net.

The old battle hymn "We Shall Not be Moved" echoed around the terraces. Everton were home, dry and deserved Champions.

Everton had man-of-the-match contenders in all the key departments as they swept to glory against QPR.

Graeme Sharp was an impressive figure up front, and central midfielders Paul Bracewell and Peter Reid dominated the centre of the park.

The final vote went to Reid, a player whose inspirational play has excited the fans all season, and who was once again at his best as the title returned to Goodison.

HOWARD KENDALL
– inside the dressing room

When you've got a great team, like we had in the mid-Eighties, you feel a real sense of satisfaction when you write it down before a game and hand it to the referee. As soon as the opposition saw it, I'm sure it gave us a psychological advantage.

Then the visitors would step out onto that Goodison pitch and the passion of the Evertonians would give us another major boost. Over 50,000 of them turned up for the game against Queens Park Rangers, all anticipating that the title was all but ours. They desperately wanted that crown because they had taken so much stick from the red side of the city in previous years. Blues' fans had become disillusioned, but the Milk Cup and FA Cup runs had sparked them the previous season and now the Championship itself was in our grasp.

You could sense the hope and optimism for the future. When we won the FA Cup, I stood on the pitch at Wembley and thought to myself: "No one can take this away from me now." My name would be in the record books for winning something as Everton manager. That meant a lot to me.

We travelled back on the train and Bob Paisley was on board. He'd been to the final as a guest of the FA. Bob said: "Congratulations," and I thanked him.

But I added that it had to be the first step towards proving we were the best and to do that we would have to win the League. Bob nodded. He knew exactly what I meant. I passed that on to the players when we gathered at the start of the 1984/85 season. I told them that Second Division sides win the FA Cup. That did not prove they were the best. It was not demeaning our fantastic Wembley achievement in any way. It's just that I wanted Everton to be hailed as THE top team in the country.

And so as I stood on the Everton pitch at the end of that season with our title dream unfolding before us if we beat QPR, I took great satisfaction from the fact that we had moved forward in a big way. My thoughts flashed back to the day in 1969/70 when I was an Everton player and we clinched the title on home soil three games out, beating West Brom 2-0 with goals from Colin Harvey and Alan Whittle. There were over 58,000 in the stadium that day and the atmosphere throughout the game was electric.

There was so much confidence in the team, a trait I could also sense in my Eighties Championship side. I remember Alan Ball shouting to me with about 20 minutes to go in that distinctive high voice of his: "Howard. We've won it!" I said: "Yeah, brilliant!"

It wasn't us being cocky. As a team we just had this belief in each other. I felt that belief as a manager in the players who became the most successful in Everton's long history in the Eighties. And I was so proud when we beat QPR 2-0 with goals from Derek Mountfield and Graeme Sharp.

It was nice for everybody that it was settled at Goodison, just as it was in 1970. To have been a part of both of those occasions just added to it for me.

92

1984/85 LEAGUE STATS:

Home games in bold.

AUG			
25	**Tottenham**	L 1-4 Heath (pen)	35,630
27	West Brom	L 1-2 Heath (pen)	13,464
31	Chelsea	W 1-0 Richardson	17,734
SEP			
4	**Ipswich**	**D 1-1 Heath**	22,314
8	**Coventry**	**W 2-1 Sharp, Steven**	20,013
15	Newcastle	W 3-2 Gray, Sheedy, Steven	26,944
22	**Southampton**	**D 2-2 Mountfield, Sharp**	22,354
29	Watford	W 5-4 Heath 2, Mountfield, Sharp, Steven	15,253
OCT			
6	Arsenal	W 0-1	37,949
13	**Aston Villa**	**W 2-1 Heath, Sharp**	25,089
20	Liverpool	W 1-0 Sharp	45,545
27	**Man Utd**	**W 5-0 Sheedy 2, Heath, Sharp, Stevens**	40,769
NOV			
3	Leicester	W 3-0 Heath, Sheedy, Steven	27,784
10	West Ham	W 1-0 Heath	24,089
17	**Stoke**	**W 4-0 Heath 2, Reid, Steven**	26,705
24	Norwich	L 2-4 Sharp, Sheedy	16,925
DEC			
1	**Sheffield Wed**	**D 1-1 Sharp (pen)**	35,440
8	QPR	D 0-0	14,338
15	**Nottm Forest**	**W 5-0 Sharp 2, Reid, Sheedy, Steven**	22,487
22	Chelsea	L 3-4 Sharp 2 pens, Bracewell	29,887
26	Sunderland	W 2-1 Mountfield 2	19,714
29	Ipswich T.	W 2-0 Sharp 2	16,045

JAN			
1	Luton	W 2-1 Steven 2	31,682
12	Newcastle	W 4-0 Sheedy 2, Mountfield, Sharp	32,156
FEB			
2	Watford	W 4-0 Stevens 2, Sheedy, Steven	27,026
23	Leicester	W 2-1 Gray 2	17,345
MAR			
2	Man Utd	D 1-1 Mountfield	51,150
16	Aston Villa	D 1-1 Richardson	22,625
23	**Arsenal**	**W 2-0 Gray, Sharp**	27,389
30	Southampton	W 2-1 Richardson 2	18,754
APRIL			
3	Tottenham	W 2-1 Gray, Steven	48,108
6	Sunderland	W 4-1 Gray 2, Sharp, Steven	35,978
16	West Brom	W 4-1 Sharp 2 (one pen), Atkin, Sheedy	29,750
20	Stoke City	W 2-0 Sharp, Sheedy	9,285
27	**Norwich**	**W 3-0 Bracewell, Mountfield, Steven**	32,085
MAY			
4	Sheff Wed.	W 1-0 Gray	37,381
6	**QPR**	**W 2-0 Mountfield, Sharp**	50,514
8	**West Ham**	**W 3-0 Mountfield 2, Gray**	32,657
11	Notts Forest	L 0-1	18,784
23	**Liverpool**	**W 1-0 Wilkinson**	51,045
26	Coventry	L 1-4 Wilkinson	21,224
28	Luton Town	L 0-2	11,509

Final League position: First in Division One.

FIVE STAR:
Derek Mountfield shows his opposite number from QPR how it's done in this May, 1984 league game

BAYERN BLITZED: Andy Gray watches the ball enter the net

The Match...

BAYERN BLITZED IN GOODISON CAULDRON

EVERTON 3 BAYERN MUNICH 1
European Cup Winners Cup, Semi-Final, Second Leg, April 24, 1985

Everton: Southall, Stevens, Van den Hauwe, Ratcliffe, Mountfield, Reid, Steven, Sharp, Gray, Bracewell, Sheedy.
Bayern Munich: Pfaff, Dremmler, Willmer (Belerlorzer 66), Eder (Rummenigge 74), Augenthaler, Lerby, Pflugler, Matthaus, Hoeness, Nachtweth, Kogl.
Referee: Mr. E. Fredriksson (Sweden).
Goals: Hoeness 27, Sharp 68, Gray 73, Steven 84. Everton win 3-1 on aggregate.
Bookings: Gray (Everton), Pflugler (Bayern).
Attendance: 49,476.

By Ken Rogers

EVERTON gave one of the greatest club sides in Europe a one goal start last night and then battered them into submission to power into the Cup Winners Cup Final.

Goodison Park exploded as goals from Graeme Sharp, Andy Gray and Trevor Steven broke the hearts of Bayern Munich. The West German league leaders thought they had the semi-final in the bag when Dieter Hoeness squeezed them in front after 27 minutes.

But Everton, inspired by 11 heroes on the pitch and 49,000 never-say-die supporters on the terraces, hit back with a vengeance to clinch a famous victory and a final place in Rotterdam against Rapid Vienna on May 15.

The courage, determination and commitment that inspired this triumph was epitomised in the displays of Everton's three goalscorers.

Sharp and Gray gave the Germans a pounding with as good a display as you will see. It was the very best of British in terms of bold and aggressive centre-forward play and the reward was a goal apiece in the second half when Bayern were on the rack and on the run as the Blues seized control.

If that wasn't enough, Steven brought the house down four minutes from time like some latter-day Bobby Charlton, racing clear and unleashing an unstoppable shot from the edge of the box that flew past Belgian international keeper Jean-Marie Pfaff to make it 3-1.

The final whistle came with the Goodison fans roaring out a deafening salute on a night when Merseyside had two teams to be proud of in Europe.

Skipper Kevin Ratcliffe rushed across to throw his arms around his Welsh international team mate Neville Southall and every player received a standing ovation as he moved down the tunnel.

Last off was Gray, savouring every second of the excitement. He thrust his fists high into the air and the final cheer must have rattled the Bayern dressing-room door as the Germans reflected bitterly on a remarkable game.

The first half was a full-blooded, no-holds-barred affair that bubbled like a volcano at times as the Munich outfit tried to stem the Everton charge.

In Hans Pflugler they had a hit-man who infuriated the home fans as he twice sent Sharp crashing and then turned his attentions to Gray.

The Scot kicked out wildly in retaliation, an unfortunate rush of blood that could have proved costly, but he escaped with a caution, and Pflugler joined him in the book. In terms of chances Everton had totally dominated the action and Steven should have broken the deadlock after four minutes, snatching at a close range cross and screwing the ball wide.

Bayern had managed just a single shot on target when they suddenly stunned the Blues with the kind of swift break that was always a nagging possibility.

Golden boy Ludwig Kugl found himself in the clear, and although Southall blocked his shot on the edge of the box, Hoeness followed up to squeeze the ball home between two defenders on the line.

Three minutes into the second half, Everton hit back when Gray knocked on a long Gary Stevens throw and Sharp pounced for his 29th goal of the season, a glancing header that set up a storming finish. Another Stevens throw had Bayern at sixes and sevens after 75 minutes, with Pfaff failing to hold the ball and seeming to be impeded by two of his own players on the line. Gray scooped the ball home first time to send the fans wild with excitement.

Steven turned the screw in the 86th minute and you won't see a sweeter build-up or a more decisive piece of finishing. Sheedy started it with a superb through-ball. Gray's boot flicked it on, beyond his marker Nachtweth, and Steven advanced to wipe out the Germans in style.

 **★ STAR MAN**

It is difficult to name a man-of-the-match when a team has eleven heroes, but on a night when Everton had to show all their fighting qualities to move through to the final, Andy Gray and Graeme Sharp had to be major contenders. Trevor Steven's skill and pace also outshone German star Ludwig Kugl, but the verdict went to Gray - a giant up front and the man who never let Bayern relax for a single moment.

HOWARD KENDALL
– inside the dressing room

Before you assess this particular classic, you have to think about the first leg in Munich. The way we set about the challenge was tremendous and the goalless draw was well deserved. I remember going to the Press Conference afterwards. Bayern coach Udo Lattek was sitting back in his chair, looking almost smug because we had not secured an away goal. That was his mentality. He possibly thought they were the best team in the competition and was clearly confident that they could score at Goodison.

When they did, after 27 minutes, he definitely believed they were one of the best teams in Europe and on their way to the final. He knew we would have to score two with an hour to go and the Germans were full of confidence at that point.

But the passion of the players and the atmosphere in the stadium told our bench that we were far from beaten. I would say that the passion got us the first two goals, scored by Sharp and Gray, as we edged in front. The quality brought about the killer punch from Trevor Steven.

I had played in Cup Finals and played at all the great grounds in the country, but Goodison that night was something very special. I had never witnessed an atmosphere like it, before or since. Those who were there - players, staff and fans - were privileged. None of us will ever forget it. Our dug-out was packed. Everyone just wanted to be part of the occasion. When it was finally all over I went out for a meal.

I got home in the early hours and then watched it all over again on video. The kids were coming down to go to school and I was still looking at it. Little things stick in your mind. We were battering them into submission and Lattek shouted across to our bench: "Kendall, this is not football!" We leapt up as one and shouted back in unison: "F*** O**!!"

When the bedlam finally calmed down, Lattek showed a different face. He came across and said: "Good luck in the final."

As I said, they thought they were amongst the best in Europe. Now we knew that we were in that elite group and nothing was going to stop us.

HERE WE GO: Trevor Steven pounces

FAN-TASTIC WELCOME: The Everton support has always been passionate. Here Peter Reid and Adrian Heath taste that Blue Pride

The Match...

DIFFERENT CLASS ON A EURO STAGE

EVERTON 3 RAPID VIENNA 1
European Cup Winners Cup Final, May 15, 1985

EVERTON (4-4-2): Southall, Stevens, Mountfield, Ratcliffe, Van den Hauwe, Steven, Reid, Bracewell, Sheedy, Sharp, Gray. Subs: Arnold, Bailey, Harper, Richardson, Atkins.
RAPID VIENNA (4-4-2): Konsel, Lainer, Brauneder, Weber, Garger, Kranjcar, Kienast, Hrstic, Pacuit (Gross), Krankl, Winhofer (Paneka).
GOALS: Gray (Everton) 37 mins. 1-0; Steven (Everton) 72 mins. 2-0; Krankl (Rapid) 83 mins. 2-1; Sheedy (Everton) 86 mins. 3-1.
CORNERS: Everton 10. Rapid 2.
BOOKINGS: Weber (Rapid) and Stevens (Everton) both for fouls.
REFEREE: Mr. Paolo Casarin of Italy.
ATTENDANCE: Estimated 45,000.

By Ian Hargraves

MAGNIFICENT! That is the only word to describe Everton's performance in over-running Rapid Vienna in Rotterdam last night to claim their first European trophy. Rapid's former Golden Boot winner Hans Krankl summed it all up when he said: "Everton were just too good for us. It is a very long time since we played against anyone of their class.

"In all our other games in Europe we have been given the chance to win at some time, but Everton gave us no chance at all."

Krankl's words are an accurate description of a match that Everton dominated. They put enormous pressure on their opponents right from the start and had so many attacking options that Rapid never knew where the next attack was coming from.

Few teams since the war have given such a complete demonstration of all-out, controlled football. Wolves, Spurs, the pre-Munich Busby Babes and more recently one or two of Liverpool's very best teams, may have matched it from time to time; none have surpassed it.

If Kevin Sheedy and Trevor Steven were not swinging over centres for Andy Gray and Graeme Sharp, Peter Reid and Paul

Bracewell were threading passes through the middle.

And right behind them was young Derek Mountfield, powering from the back at every opportunity, and adding to the general unease surrounding goalkeeper Michael Konsel. For a side at the end of a testing season it was a remarkable achievement.

Everton's dominance on the pitch was matched by their supporters off it. The 25,000 fans who turned Rotterdam into a cauldron of noise in the morning and who entertained the locals with their humour and their footballing expertise during a series of impromptu matches in the city centre, also set the stadium rocking with their vocal support during and after the match. Rapid's green-clad supporters were hopelessly out-shouted.

Given such a reception, it was unthinkable the Blues should lose, and the only surprise was that they did not wrap it all up well before the interval. In the opening 20 minutes Rapid barely crossed the halfway line as Everton came at them from all angles. Konsel beat out a fierce right footer from Sheedy while Bracewell fired a shot only inches wide.

Gray actually netted in 39 minutes, after Mountfield had headed a Sheedy free-kick back inside, and though the whistle went for offside, it must have been desperately close.

Rapid caused a few flutters of unease on the resumption when Pat Van den Hauwe was forced to head a Kranjcar shot against his own cross bar and Kevin Ratcliffe intervened at the last moment to foil Krankl, but once Gray had put Everton in front in the 57th minute the match was as good as over.

Sharp's speed of anticipation enabled him to beat Konsel to a poor back-pass and his squared pass was volleyed into the empty net by a delighted Gray.

Steven almost increased the lead when he turned his man superbly at the end of an intricate move involving half a dozen players, only to see his shot saved by Konsel, but made amends by adding the second goal after 72 minutes.

Rapid's defence were all at sea as Sheedy curled in a typical corner, and the ball flew straight through to Steven who could hardly miss.

Understandably, Everton then relaxed, and although they suffered a minor shock when Krankl snatched a goal back after rounding Neville Southall, they re-emphasised their dominance by scoring again immediately.

Straight from the kick-off they swept downfield with almost contemptuous ease, and Sharp's diagonal pass set Sheedy free to hammer the ball home.

That goal put the finishing touch to a memorable performance. Not only had Everton shown their ability to beat a top Continental side, but they had done so with the kind of style now associated with the modern Goodison.

You can't ask for more than that!

The Everton team all played well and it was hard to single out individuals. However, the midfield was outstanding with Peter Reid and Paul Bracewell demonstrating just why they have been brought together in the England squad. Bracewell came into his own in the second half especially, but Reid's first half performance was superb. His use of the ball and imagination were a joy to watch and he gets the verdict.

HOWARD KENDALL
– inside the dressing room

I was very confident about the final against Rapid, but I tried not to show it to the players. We had overshadowed one of the best teams in Europe in the semi-final and we had to be favourites to claim the trophy.

But I did not want the players to feel that it was a formality. We still had to go out there and impose ourselves and our opponents had at least one world-class player in giant striker Hans Krankl.

I had been to Vienna to see Rapid and I did not feel we had a problem - apart from him! I still prepared our lads with a warning that they were a good side, but the confidence within our squad was massive. When you look at opponents and the way they do things, set pieces are very important, particularly when you are assessing possible weaknesses.

I noticed that they often failed to cover at the far post when defending free-kicks. In Kevin Sheedy, we had someone who could exploit that with his accurate crosses. Trevor Steven came in round the back to net our second and that pleased me as a manager.

Yes, we can applaud the spectacular shot or header, but when you pinpoint something before a game and it proves correct, you feel a sense of satisfaction. All successes are special, but when it's a first it is extra special. Everton had never won a European trophy before and I was full of pride as we edged towards that dream. With the score at 2-0 thanks to Gray and Steven, I came down from the stand to the dug-out.

I wanted to be there, close to the lads, when the final whistle signalled our victory. A little Dutch radio journalist came across to the bench, holding out his microphone. The game still had eight minutes to go, but he had decided we were home and dry.

He said: "Kendall, what does it feel like to win the European Cup Winners Cup?"

Normally I would have brushed aside any journalist in that situation, but the whole stadium was focused on an Everton victory and I turned away for a split second with that microphone thrust in my face and said: "Er. . . "

Before I could get a single word out there was an Austrian roar and I looked beyond this little Dutchman to see Krankl turning away after scoring.

I jumped up and pointed my finger in the face of the interviewer. He fully understood the two words I spat out, the second one being OFF! It was now 2-1 and I was on my feet as we kicked off again. In a flash the ball was down at their end and Kevin Sheedy stuck it in the back of their net.

I looked round for my Dutch friend and spotted him. "YOU," I shouted. He wondered what was coming next, but his worried look turned to a smile when I said: "Come here. I'll talk to you now!"

We both beamed as the whistle went. The Cup was ours. What a night. What a season.

1984/85 EUROPEAN CUP WINNERS CUP STATS

Home fixtures in bold.

ROUND	DATE	TEAM	RESULT
1 (1st Leg)	Sept 19	UC Dublin	D 0-0
1 (2nd Leg)	**Oct 2**	**UC Dublin**	**W 1-0 (agg 1-0) Sharp**
2 (1st Leg)	Oct 24	Inter Bratislava	W 1-0 Bracewell
2 (2nd Leg)	**Nov 7**	**Inter Bratislava**	**W 3-0 (agg 4-0) Heath, Sheedy, Sharp**
3 (1st Leg)	**Mar 6**	**Fortuna Sittard**	**W 3-0 Gray 3**
3 (2nd Leg)	Mar 20	Fortuna Sittard	W 2-0 (agg 5-0) Reid, Sharp
SF (1st Leg)	Apr 10	Bayern Munich	D 0-0
SF (2nd Leg)	**Apr 24**	**Bayern Munich**	**W 3-1 (agg 3-1) Gray, Sharp, Steven**
*Final	May 15	Rapid Vienna	W 3-1 Gray, Sheedy, Steven

*At Rotterdam

1984/1985 ENGLISH DIVISION 1 TABLE

	P	HW	HD	HL	HGF	HGA	AW	AD	AL	AGF	AGA	Pts	GD
Everton	42	16	3	2	58	17	12	3	6	30	26	**90**	+45
Liverpool	42	12	4	5	36	19	10	7	4	32	16	**77**	+33
Tottenham	42	11	3	7	46	31	12	5	4	32	20	**77**	+27
Man Utd	42	13	6	2	47	13	9	4	8	30	34	**76**	+30
Southampton	42	13	4	4	29	18	6	7	8	27	29	**68**	+9
Chelsea	42	13	3	5	38	20	5	9	7	25	28	**66**	+15
Arsenal	42	14	5	2	37	14	5	4	12	24	35	**66**	+12
Sheff Wed	42	12	7	2	39	21	5	7	9	19	24	**65**	+13
Nottm Forest	42	13	4	4	35	18	6	3	12	21	30	**64**	+8
Aston Villa	42	10	7	4	34	20	5	4	12	26	40	**56**	0
Watford	42	10	5	6	48	30	4	8	9	33	41	**55**	+10
West Brom	42	11	4	6	36	23	5	3	13	22	39	**55**	-4
Luton	42	12	5	4	40	22	3	4	14	17	39	**54**	-4
Newcastle	42	11	4	6	33	26	2	9	10	22	44	**52**	-15
Leicester	42	10	4	7	39	25	5	2	14	26	48	**51**	-8
West Ham	42	7	8	6	27	23	6	4	11	24	45	**51**	-17
Ipswich	42	8	7	6	27	20	5	4	12	19	37	**50**	-11
Coventry	42	11	3	7	29	22	4	2	15	18	42	**50**	-17
QPR	42	11	6	4	41	30	2	5	14	12	42	**50**	-19
Norwich	42	9	6	6	28	24	4	4	13	18	40	**49**	-18
Sunderland	42	7	6	8	20	26	3	4	14	20	36	**40**	-22
Stoke	42	3	3	15	18	41	0	5	16	6	50	**17**	-67

WATCH OUT, ANDY:
Peter Reid can't hide
his elation at Gray's
crucial Cup Winners
Cup Final goal
against Rapid
Vienna. Reidy's
flying leap reflects
the importance of
Andy's strike.
Graeme Sharp holds
his Scottish team
mate aloft

STARTING POINT: Andy King shoots against Coventry in that crucial Milk Cup clash in 1983. The ball eventually fell to Adrian Heath who scored to help prevent a potential disaster for the Blues

LOCAL AND PROUD OF IT: John Bailey shows the pride and passion for which he was famous

GIVE US A SMILE, BOYS: John Bailey, Adrian Heath, Derek Mountfield, Alan Irvine and Kevin Ratcliffe strike a happy pose

AGONY AND ECSTASY:
And no prizes for guessing who is on the up and up. Graeme Sharp turns away in delight after Andy King's Milk Cup goal against West Ham in December, 1983

FLYING HIGH: Peter Reid takes to the air to join in a goal celebration. A familiar sight in the 80's. This was against Oxford in the Milk Cup in January, 1984

HEROES AND VILLAINS: Alan Irvine jumps with Villa's Nigel Spink during the Milk Cup semi-final at Villa Park in February, 1984

TEAM HUG: Kevin Sheedy's the centre of attention after scoring against Aston Villa in the League Cup semi-final in February, 1984

A LITTLE SMASHER:
Adrian Heath's getting
ruffled, but he looks
more than happy

**PUTTING THE
BOOT IN:**
The left one, of
course, as Kevin
Sheedy launches
another pinpoint
cross into the box.
The game is
Oxford, Milk Cup,
January 1984

HE'S HERE, HE'S THERE, HE'S EVERYWHERE: Adrian Heath scores versus Chesterfield in a 1983 Milk Cup tie (right) and is pictured in action (below) against Aston Villa at Goodison in February, 1984

STEP OVER: Kevin Sheedy scores against West Ham in the Milk Cup at Goodison in December, 1983

SILOUETTE OF A CLASSIC STRIKER: Andy King (left) scores the first against West Ham in the Milk Cup, December, 1983

SUPER SALUTE: Messrs Ratcliffe, Sheedy and Sharp acknowledge the fans (right) as they celebrate victory at Villa in the Milk Cup, semi-final, second leg in February, 1984

SHOOTING STARS: Clockwise, it's Sharp against Oxford in 1984; Richardson scoring against Aston Villa in the Milk Cup and (below) Heath and Sharp both hitting the bar in the second leg at Villa Park

POWER TO YOUR ELBOW:
Graeme Sharp takes a knock, from Villa's Alan Evans, but had the last laugh in the Milk Cup semi-final as the Blues moved through

TEN OUT OF TEN:
Alan Irvine lets the fans know that the players truly appreciate them after the 1984 Milk Cup semi-final triumph at Villa Park

GETTING THERE FIRST: Graeme Sharp puts Aston Villa under pressure in the Milk Cup semi-final, second leg

SNOW PLACE LIKE HOME: Kevin Richardson scores in the Milk Cup, fifth round replay victory over Oxford

United after surviving that famous scare away from home

THE ORIGINAL HUDDLE: These celebrations followed Kevin Richardson's goal to make it 2-0 against Aston Villa in the first leg of the Milk Cup semi-final at Goodison Park in February, 1984

125

RICHO'S REWARD: Kevin emerges from the pack, clearly delighted after that goal against Villa

SUPER SHEEDY: Kevin (partly hidden, left) rifles home against Oxford in the Milk Cup replay on January 24, 1984

THAT WINNING FEELING:
We never tired of seeing Inchy's victory run, this time after his winning goal against Spurs at Goodison in January, 1984

THAT WINNING FEELING: Sheeds is centre stage after scoring in the 1984 Oxford replay

KINGY'S DELIGHT: Andy King makes his way through the fans after Everton confirmed their Milk Cup Final place at Aston Villa in February, 1984

DID WE WIN? The faces suggest it was another good day. A young Neville Southall and Alan Irvine beam with delight

Howard's Love Affair...

NOT JUST A GREAT MANAGER: We couldn't resist slotting in this famous Howard Kendall moment after he scored the winner in the
Goodison derby against Liverpool in February, 1968. Joe Royle leaps with delight while Reds' skipper Ron Yeats looks on in anguish

FLYING HIGH: Andy Gray shares a joke with Adrian Heath and Howard Kendall en route to a 1985 Cup Winners Cup challenge

CHEERS TO ANOTHER TROPHY SUCCESS:
The most successful Everton manager of all time

WINNING WAYS: Another Manager of the Month award

SUPER PARTNERSHIP: Howard and Colin Harvey

TASH-TASTIC: Howard lifting the cup

NO, IT'S NOT INCHY DRESSED UP:
It's Howard and a young Bellefield guest. Ten year old Barrie Hill from Bromborough (right) was invited to spend the day at Bellefield in March, 1986, after winning a "Life At The Top" competition organised by the Boys' Brigade.
Barrie immediately declared that he wanted Howard's job, to the amusement of Paul Wilkinson and Derek Mountfield.
Where are you now, Barrie?

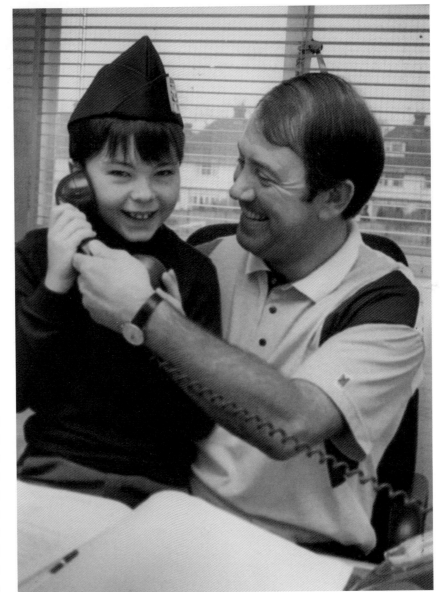

PHONE FUN:
Young Barrie Hill rings his mates to tell them about his VIP day at Bellefield with Champion boss Howard Kendall and the Everton players

MANAGER OF THE MONTH:
Howard would go on and win two Manager of the Year awards in the Eighties

MANAGERS WITH A WEMBLEY CHALLENGE: Liverpool's Joe Fagan has a few thoughts for his young rival under the Twin Towers at the Milk Cup Final in 1984

ALL ANGLES COVERED: Howard, Colin Harvey and Mick Heaton down in the dug-out

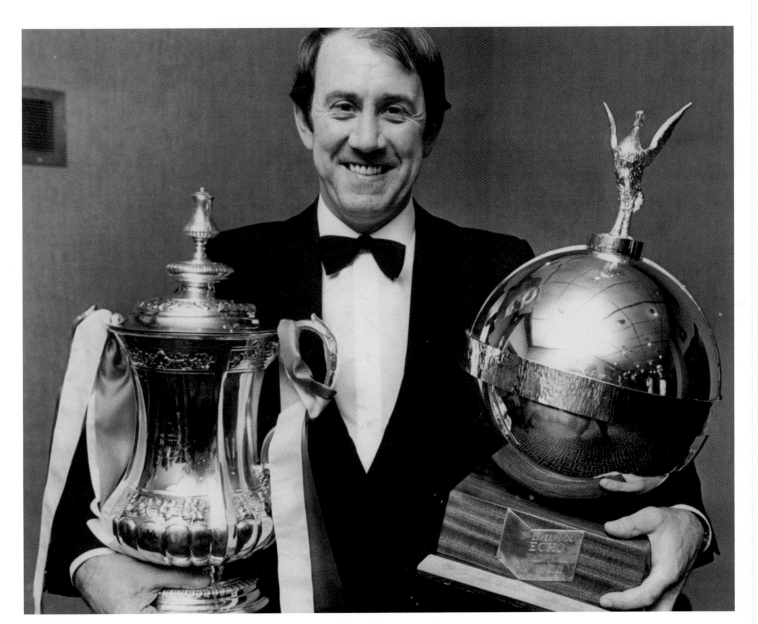

SILVER SUPER HERO: Howard with the FA Cup and the Echo's Merseyside Sports Personality of the Year award. He won the latter as an Everton player and claimed it again as a manager in 1984

**IT CAN BE A
SERIOUS GAME:**
But the smiles were
never far away
during that glorious
mid-Eighties era

EL KEL AND EL TEL: That's Howard and Terry Darracott who had a spell on the backroom staff

TIME TO WORK-OUT: Howard takes an early training session at Goodison

WATCH OUT BOB: Howard has won his first trophy, the FA Cup in 1984, and on the train back to Merseyside it's worth reminding the old enemy that the resurgent Blues are on the march. Liverpool legend Bob Paisley had been a guest of the FA at Wembley

TOWN HALL CELEBRATION: Howard Kendall and Kevin Ratcliffe parade the Charity Shield, Canon League trophy and European Cup Winners Cup at a Liverpool Town Hall gathering in 1985

147

TOP BOSS:
The Manager of
the Year award
was in Howard's
hands twice. This
was his 1987
triumph

85/86 Oh so close

1985/86 WAS A HIGHLY EVENTFUL SEASON, BUT AT THE END OF IT HOWARD KENDALL AND HIS PLAYERS HAD NOTHING TO SHOW FOR THEIR GALLANT EFFORTS. BUT HOW DO YOU JUDGE SUCCESS? BY ANYBODY'S HIGH STANDARDS, THIS WAS ANOTHER REMARKABLE YEAR FOR THE BLUES.

At the end of it, just two key games cost Everton an historic League and FA Cup double. Perhaps it was the unpalatable fact that it was Liverpool who snatched the glory that makes this a campaign some Evertonians would possibly prefer to discount or even blot from the memory banks.

But it would be tragic to dismiss or diminish the efforts of Kendall's men in this pulsating season that was the prelude to yet further title success in 1987.

In tried and trusted fashion, the manager once again proved that he could take the toughest of decisions. In the summer of '85, he decided to part company with the Scottish striker who had become a real fans' idol - Andy Gray.

The centre-forward had won over the crowd on day one and he had never let them down with his fearless front running and ability to go in where others feared to tread. But Gray had arrived with injury problems and it was questionable how long he could power on. That does not mean he held anything back in any situation. It's just that Kendall and his right-hand man Colin Harvey knew that to win trophies and then to go out and win some more, you have to seek the best available.

Leicester's free-scoring England star Gary Lineker was certainly in that category and he was up for grabs, having gone as far as he could at Filbert Street. Everton decided he was the man to help them maintain their momentum. Lineker arrived in the June, despite the clubs failing to agree on a fee. The Blues came in at £400,000. Leicester demanded £1.25m. A transfer tribunal subsequently settled on £800,000. It would be another month before Gray would leave Goodison, returning to one of his former clubs Aston Villa.

One short, but momentous Goodison career was over. Could another one now explode into life? Lineker faced an intriguing debut, at the club he had just turned his back on. Unhappily, it was a day of double disappointment for the new man. Everton lost 3-1 and their only goal came from a defender, not a striker, although Derek Mountfield was not unaccustomed to finding the back of the net. The Champions found top gear at home where an Adrian Heath double was good enough to overshadow West Brom. Graeme Sharp was the lone goal hit man in a subsequent 1-1 home draw with another Midlands outfit, Coventry City.

But Lineker soon demonstrated his star quality with goals in three successive games. He grabbed the winner at Tottenham, conjured up a magnificent treble in a 4-1 rout of Birmingham and then struck two more goals in a 5-1 triumph at Sheffield Wednesday. No one was going to forget Gray in a hurry, but with Heath, Sharp and Lineker amongst the goals in the opening six games, it seemed that boss Kendall had struck pure gold.

One thing that was clear was that Everton were playing a fundamentally different game with the fast and direct England star leading the line. Lineker managed just one goal in the following nine outings, during which time the title holders only managed three victories. There was no doubting Lineker's supreme ability in front of goal, but after that good start, he was now taking a little time to settle.

In typical fashion, he exploded into life again to dispel any questions about his own individual ability. Two goals in a 6-1 home win over Arsenal had the Goodison faithful roaring his name again. Gary's individual tally began to rise and it was impressive to say the least, but the goals were not being shared out as they had been the previous year.

The Championship midfield had only played five league games together during the course of the season. Kendall watched his new star with admiration, but he began to wonder if the man up front was too much of a magnet for the direct ball. Still, the Blues were well placed to challenge powerfully once more for the Championship crown. They had fallen in the fourth round of the League Cup against Chelsea after beating Bournemouth and Shrewsbury. Lineker had picked up three goals in the five games. Everton had fared even better in the FA Cup and Exeter, Blackburn, Spurs, Luton and Sheffield Wednesday would all be vanquished as the Blues returned to what was becoming their second home, Wembley Stadium.

The bonus was another all-Merseyside final, this time in the premier domestic Cup competition. But the priority remained the League and what a battle it was becoming with Liverpool also retaining powerful title ambitions. Three games out, Everton went to Oxford where Lineker, by his own high standards, had one of those days when nothing would go right. The Blues lost 1-0 and suddenly the initiatve was with the Mersey Reds. Even though Gary bounced back with a hat-trick in a 6-1 thrashing of Southampton, Kendall now knew that he had to rely on his arch-rivals slipping up with the finishing line in sight.

Everton finished on a high note, thumping West Ham 3-1 at Goodison. Lineker's double took his league tally to a remarkable 30 goals with ten more plundered in the cups. It was good enough to earn him aboth the Footballer of the Year accolade and the vote of his peers in the PFA Awards. It was not enough to help Everton keep the title and the pain was accentuated at the double as Liverpool took that honour, as well as coming from behind under the Twin Towers to claim the Cup 3-1.

How close can you get to an historic FA Cup and League double? It was agonising, but no one should underplay Everton's heroic efforts. Graeme Sharp had plundered 19 league goals himself, but Sheedy had to settle for five against 11 the previous year. Steven had nine against 12, including four pens. Heath's ten against 11 was comparable, but of the 85 goals amassed only two men got more than ten - Lineker and Sharp. In the Championship year, Heath, Sharp, Sheedy, Steven and Mountfield had all achieved that.

The difference between success and failure was miniscule, but it was enough to force boss Kendall to make one of the toughest decisions of his managerial career.

Lineker, having achieved world-class status in Mexico with England in the summer where his six goals made him leading scorer, was sacrificed for the wider good. He joined Barcelona in what was then a massive £2.5m deal.

Everton would regroup for the 1986/87 campaign. Had the club's highly respected manager made the right call? We would soon find out.

HEADING FOR THE INTERVAL TEAM TALK:
Howard has got things on his mind and Paul Bracewell steps up the pace to get back into the dressing room

GET IT SORTED:
The boss shouts
from the dug-out
alongside physio
John Clinkard and
substitute Neil
Pointon

The Match...

MERSEY HOTSHOTS GUN DOWN ARSENAL

EVERTON 6 ARSENAL 1
League. November 9, 1985

Everton (4-4-2): Southall, Harper, Pointon, Ratcliffe, Stevens, Heath, Steven, Lineker, Sharp, Bracewell, Sheedy. Sub: Richardson.
Arsenal(4-4-2): Lukic, Anderson, Sansom, Davis, O'Leary, Caton, Williams, Allinson, Nicholas, Woodcock, Rix. Sub: Whyte.
Referee: Mr. Maurice Robinson (Sutton Coldfield).
Goals: Lineker 2 (19, 39), Heath 2 (50, 80), Steven pen (63), Sharp (84).
Attendance: 28,620.

By Ian Hargraves

THE zest that characterised last season's Championship challenge was there for all to see against Arsenal. Shortly before the end a London scribe asked if Arsenal were really as poor as they were made to appear, or if Everton were simply in unbeatable form.

Both suggestions were partly true, but from Everton's point of view they could hardly have done more than outclass the players sent against them.

Adrian Heath, Gary Lineker and Graeme Sharp made up a deadly threesome, supported strongly from midfield, while Gary Stevens fitted in at centre-back as though that were his England position.

As for young Neil Pointon, who could easily have been losing with Scunthorpe in the Fourth Division, he had a dream debut at left-back.

Long before the end he had won the hearts of a delighted Goodison crowd with his bubbling enthusiasm, determined tackling and willingness to go forward.

Although he must now return to the reserves to continue his apprenticeship, it will be a long time before he forgets the day he helped hit Arsenal for six.

Considering the Gunners boast so many high-priced players and have England's chief coach as their manager, they were remarkably ineffective.

The class of men like Charlie Nicholas, Kenny Sansom and Graham Rix was clear for everyone to see, but the side as a whole never looked more than a collection of talented individuals.

It is sometimes alleged that London teams lack the stomach for a real fight and Saturday's performance made it seem at least conceivable.

There was little commitment and far too great a willingness to sit back and admire a good pass rather than complete the job.

Admittedly, Arsenal were a little unlucky to see what looked like a perfectly good goal by Allinson disallowed only a minute or two before Gary Lineker scored his second for Everton.

It followed a long run by Nicholas and was cancelled because Woodcock was lying in an offside position, even though he was not interfering with play.

Such an upset was inevitably disappointing, but Championship contenders are expected to roll up their sleeves and get stuck in at moments like that.

Everton showed how it should be done when they responded to a goal by Nicholas immediately after the interval with a first strike by Heath, who was in like a flash to finish off a move by Sharp and Lineker .

After that, Arsenal simply folded up with O'Leary and Caton all at sea against Everton's eager attackers.

Trevor Steven converted a penalty after Heath had been fouled by Davis. Heath scored his second goal to round off a superb movement built by Bracewell and Steven, and finally Sharp rounded off an excellent personal display by scoring the sixth goal from a pass by Sheedy.

There could easily have been more. O'Leary kicked off the line from two-goal Lineker who also saw a fierce header brilliantly saved by Lukic and Bracewell smacked a fine shot against the bar.

Still, six will do for starters.

 STAR MAN

All three Everton strikers played well with Lineker and Heath getting a couple of goals each and Sharp also scoring. Another outstanding display came from Gary Stevens who had an excellent match at centre-back. He has played there once or twice before and seemed just as much at home there as in his normal right-back slot. He gets the verdict.

HOWARD KENDALL
– inside the dressing room

That emphatic victory over Arsenal came in a season that some might deem a failure, but certainly not me. We were just two games away from an historic double which is a great campaign in any situation. The real problem was that the double was won by our neighbours.

But if we had finished runners-up now, we would have been in the Champions League with all that entails. As it was, we could so easily have retained the title we won so magnificently the year before.

Most clubs in the country would have swopped places with us that year, but it shows how much of an edge there is between the great Mersey rivals.

The thing I remember about the Arsenal game was Neil Pointon's debut. I naturally reflect on a Gary Lineker double and the controversy that would follow later when he was transferred to Barcelona after racking up 40 goals that season. I still believe it was the right decision, based on my belief that it is crucial that goals come from all areas, not just one main source.

Okay, you are all going to jump up and shout, "DIXIE DEAN - 60 in one record-breaking season." Lineker fell 20 short of becoming a Goodison legend and persuading me to keep him! I say that tongue in cheek, of course. No one can take away Gary's personal input in 1985/86 which was magnificent.

He was criticised when we lost a crucial league game at Oxford just three matches out with the title in our sights. We don't need reminding that Liverpool won against Leicester that day to seize the championship initiative. But any such criticism was outrageous. Yes, Gary missed some chances in the game, but you can't knock any striker who finishes with 40!

All you will get from me is praise for Lineker's contribution. But I repeat my wider view that you must look at the overall picture. I remain convinced that you can't play to one particular style and Gary, because of his pace and directness, inadvertently imposed that on us.

Next time I see him, I'll mention Dixie. Another 20 was not too much to ask, was it? It could have changed history even further. Seriously, Gary Lineker was a great striker and played his part in an eventful season that is only overshadowed because it slots between two famous title years.

THUMBS UP:
It's the
unstoppable
Gary Lineker
looking mean
and moody.
Someone must
have stolen his
crisps!

The Match...

GARY'S GOLDEN BOOTS CRUSH THE SAINTS

EVERTON 6 SOUTHAMPTON 1
League, May 3rd 1986

Everton: Mimms, Stevens, Van den Hauwe, Ratcliffe, Mountfield, Reid, Steven, Lineker, Sharp, Bracewell, Sheedy.
Sub: Heath.
Southampton: Granger, Forrest, Tankard, Case, Gittens, Whitlock, Townsend, Cockerill, Lawrence, Armstrong, Wallace. Sub: Puckett.
Referee: Mr. P. Willis (County Durham).
Goals: Lineker 3 (30, 34, 62), Mountfield (10), Steven (29), Sharp (52).
Attendance: 33,057.

By Ken Rogers

EVERTON ran riot at Goodison Park this afternoon where a Gary Lineker hat-trick helped to inflict a crushing defeat on Southampton.
With England goalkeeper Peter Shilton injured and deputy Phil Kite away on loan at Middlesbrough, the Saints gave a baptism of fire to youth team player Keith Granger. The 17-year old was on a hiding to nothing, the Blues taking the lead after 10 minutes and securing a four-goal advantage by the interval.

Derek Mountfield, Trevor Steven and Lineker were the men on the mark in this amazing spell. The players tried to keep their minds on the job in hand, Graeme Sharp increasing the lead after the break and Lineker securing his hat-trick.

The Saints, fielding a team that was a strange mixture of experience and raw youth, had a chance in the first minute when the speedy Wallace broke towards the edge of the box before testing Bobby Mimms with a low shot.

The Goodison crowd roared their side forward and immediately Gary Stevens tried to test young Granger with a lofted free-kick, the youngster catching safely above his head to get an early confidence booster.

But with Everton determined to cash-in and go for goals, the break came after just ten minutes.

It was another Stevens free-kick that put the visitors under pressure and when Granger was only able to parry a solid Graeme Sharp header, Derek Mountfield and Lineker closed in, with the big centre-half turning the ball home.

Tankard was then booked for a foul on Steven in what was an extremely hectic opening spell.

Wallace found Lawrence and it took an outstanding save from Mimms to keep Everton in front. Kevin Ratcliffe was then booked for a foul on Lawrence, and the Goodison outfit turned up the heat when Steven increased the lead after 29 minutes.

Lineker was the creator on the left, shrugging off Whitlock and getting in a superb cross that was met by the in-running Steven who glanced a header beyond Granger and into the net.

A minute later the crowd roared when Everton made it 3-0 with a goal from Lineker. Steven found the England striker who clipped the ball home from close range with Southampton on the rack and their young youth team keeper devastated.

As the visitors tried to dig-in, Townsend was booked, but Everton came forward once more with Lineker thrilling the fans by grabbing his second, and the Blues fourth, after 34 minutes.

It was Paul Bracewell who worked the ball to his team-mate and Lineker cracked it past the helpless keeper from 12 yards for his 36th strike of the season.

Incredibly, Southampton had the chances to reduce the arrears as the interval approached. First Mimms was forced to beat out a rocket shot from Case. Then Wallace swerved an effort high and wide, but it had been Everton's half with the Saints' inexperience at the back punished severely.

Bracewell failed to appear after the interval, replaced in midfield by Adrian Heath. The Blues moved straight onto the offensive with Lineker almost claiming his hat-trick when he hooked a shot from 12 yards into the arms of Granger.

Sharp then pounced to make it 5-0 after 52 minutes. Kevin Sheedy set the chance up with a pinpoint cross from the left. The Scottish striker rose majestically to power a header wide of Granger's right hand with the visitors in complete disarray.

The Saints had kicked off without four recognised defenders. Left-back Tankard, just 16, had figured in just two previous games while central defender Gittins, 21, was turning out for Paget Rangers in non-league football a few months ago. Added to this, the total inexperience of goalkeeper Granger meant that Southampton were in trouble every time the Blues attacked.

A day to forget was compounded for Gittins when he went off injured, to be replaced by Puckett whose arrival was to prove extremely timely for the Saints who suddenly pulled one back after 59 minutes.

Wallace set off on one of those tricky runs from the halfway line and when he found Puckett, the substitute turned a low shot past Mimms to make it 5-1.

But then Lineker secured his hat-trick in style to make it six. Pat Van den Hauwe found Heath on the left and his cross was headed home gleefully by the England man as Everton confirmed an emphatic victory.

 STAR MAN

The man-of-the-match verdict has to go to Gary Lineker. His pace and his quality in front of goal secured him a hat-trick on a day when Southampton were completely outclassed.

HOWARD KENDALL
– inside the dressing room

This emphatic victory over Southampton was deeply satisfying, yet at the same time it conjured up a certain amount of frustration as the 1986 title chase reached a climax. Gary Lineker was at the heart of it. Evertonians who had travelled to our previous match at Oxford will recall that a string of chances fell to Gary, but he just couldn't find the net in a game where his favourite boots had been left in Merseyside. We lost and when Liverpool won at Leicester, it suddenly tilted things in their favour at the top of the table. It was just one of those games when it didn't come off for our England striker.

Then we entertained the Saints in a game in which he plundered a hat-trick! It was too late. If only he'd put a couple away at Oxford and failed to score at Goodison. We would have still had far too much firepower for the weakened Saints.

It's amazing how many fans still mention that Oxford affair, but in football you often find yourself saying: "If only . . ."

We saw the real Gary Lineker against Southampton. Once again he showed us all what he was capable of and no one could argue with his tremendous final return of 40 goals.

It's just that we all remember 1985/86, not so much for Gary's goal input as for the simple fact that we were within touching distance of the double, something Everton had never achieved before. We were only denied at the death. Two games cost us, Oxford and the Cup Final against Liverpool. The fact that it was our arch-rivals celebrating the achievement and not us added to the total frustration.

But Gary scored to put us in front at Wembley and I have to repeat that his individual haul over the year was magnificent. It just pointed us towards a wider team decision and his departure.

1985/86 LEAGUE STATS:

Home games in bold.

AUG

17	Leicester	L 1-3	Mountfield	16,932
20	**West Brom**	**W 2-0**	Heath 2	26,788
24	Coventry	D 1-1	Sharp	27,691
26	**Tottenham**	**W 1-0**	Lineker	29,720
31	Birmingham	W 4-1	Lineker 3, Steven (pen)	28,066

SEP

3	Sheff Wed	W 5-1	Lineker 2, Mountfield, Steven, Heath	30,065
7	QPR	L 0-3		16,544
14	**Luton Town**	**W 2-0**	Sheedy, Sharp	26,419
21	**Liverpool**	**L 2-3**	Sharp, Lineker	51,509
28	Aston Villa	D 0-0		22,048

OCT

5	**Oxford Utd**	**W 2-0**	Sharp, Bracewell	24,553
12	Chelsea	L 1-2	Sheedy	27,634
19	**Watford**	**W 4-1**	Sharp 2, Heath, Bracewell	26,425
26	Man City	D 1-1	Heath	28,807

NOV

2	West Ham	L 1-2	Steven	23,844
9	**Arsenal**	**W 6-1**	Lineker 2, Heath 2, Steven (pen), Sharp	28,620
16	Ipswich Town	W 4-3	Heath, Sharp, Sheedy, Steven (pen)	13,910
23	**Nottm Forest**	**D 1-1**	**Bracewell**	27,860
30	Southampton	W 3-2	Lineker, Heath, Steven	16,917

DEC

7	West Brom	W 3-0	Sheedy, Van den Hauwe, Lineker	12,206

14	Leicester	L 1-2	Richardson	23,347
21	Coventry	W 3-1	Lineker 2, Sharp	11,059
26	**Man United**	**W 3-1**	Sharp 2, Lineker	42,551
28	Sheff Wed	W 3-1	Lineker 2, Stevens	41,536

JAN

1	Newcastle	D 2-2	Steven (pen), Sharp	27,820
11	QPR	W 4-3	Sharp 2, Lineker, Wilkinson	26,015
18	Birmingham	W 2-0	Lineker 2	10,502

FEB

1	**Tottenham**	**W 1-0**	Reid	33,178
11	**Man City**	**W 4-0**	Lineker 3, Sharp	30,006
22	Liverpool	W 2-0	Ratcliffe, Lineker	45,445

MAR

1	**Aston Villa**	**W 2-0**	Sharp, Lineker	32,133
16	Chelsea	D 1-1	Sheedy	30,145
22	Luton Town	L 1-2	Richardson	10,949
29	**Newcastle**	**W 1-0**	Richardson	41,116
31	Man Utd	D 0-0		51,189

APR

12	Arsenal	W 1-0	Heath	28,251
15	Watford	W 2-0	Lineker, Sharp	18,960
19	**Ipswich Town**	**W 1-0**	Sharp	39,055
26	Nottm Forest	D 0-0		30,171
30	Oxford Utd	L 0-1		13,939

MAY

3	Southampton	W 6-1	Lineker 3, Mountfield, Steven, Sharp	33,057
5	West Ham	W 3-1	Lineker 2, Steven (pen)	40,073

Final League Position: 2nd in Division One

1985/1986 ENGLISH DIVISION 1 TABLE

	P	HW	HD	HL	HGF	HGA	AW	AD	AL	AGF	AGA	PTS	GD
Liverpool	42	16	4	1	58	14	10	6	5	31	23	**88**	+52
Everton	42	16	3	2	54	18	10	5	6	33	23	**86**	+46
West Ham	42	17	2	2	48	16	9	4	8	26	24	**84**	+34
Man Utd	42	12	5	4	35	12	10	5	6	35	24	**76**	+34
Sheff Wed	42	13	6	2	36	23	8	4	9	27	31	**73**	+9
Chelsea	42	12	4	5	32	27	8	7	6	25	29	**71**	+1
Arsenal	42	13	5	3	29	15	7	4	10	20	32	**69**	+2
Nottm Forest	42	11	5	5	38	25	8	6	7	31	28	**68**	+16
Luton	42	12	6	3	37	15	6	6	9	24	29	**66**	+17
Tottenham	42	12	2	7	47	25	7	6	8	27	27	**65**	+22
Newcastle	42	12	5	4	46	31	5	7	9	21	41	**63**	-5
Watford	42	11	6	4	40	22	5	5	11	29	40	**59**	+7
QPR	42	12	3	6	33	20	3	4	14	20	44	**52**	-11
Southampton	42	10	6	5	32	18	2	4	15	19	44	**46**	-11
Man City	42	7	7	7	25	26	4	5	12	18	31	**45**	-14
Aston Villa	42	7	6	8	27	28	3	8	10	24	39	**44**	-16
Coventry	42	6	5	10	31	35	5	5	11	17	36	**43**	-23
Oxford Utd	42	7	7	7	34	27	3	5	13	28	53	**42**	-18
Leicester	42	7	8	6	35	35	3	4	14	19	41	**42**	-22
Ipswich	42	8	5	8	20	24	3	3	15	12	31	**41**	-23
Birmingham	42	5	2	14	13	25	3	3	15	17	48	**29**	-43
West Brom	42	3	8	10	21	36	1	4	16	14	53	**24**	-54

FEELING SMILES BETTER: Graeme Sharp scored some wonderful goals for Everton at Goodison Park and every one brought the same reaction. This was after netting in a 4-1 win against Watford in 1985

HEADS I WIN:
Gary Lineker
(above) against
Queens Park
Rangers in
September, 1985

NO STOPPING ME:
Once Gary (left) got
into his stride, the
floodgates opened.
This celebration was
against Birmingham
in January, 1986

IN ROUND THE BACK: Kevin Sheedy's late equaliser against Chelsea in March, 1986

**IS IT A BIRD? IS
IT A PLANE?:**
No, it's flying Gary
Lineker, doing an
Andy Gray
impersonation at
Villa Park in
September, 1985

THANKS FANS:
Paul Wilkinson,
Adrian Heath,
Bobby Mimms and
Gary Lineker
salute the fans at
the end of the
1985/86 season

TAKE NO CHANCES: The Nottingham Forest keeper punches clear with Derek Mountfield closing in. The game was in April, 1986

THE GOLDEN SHOT: The unmatchable Gary Lineker scores against Southampton in May, 1986

SWANSONG: This was Lineker's last league goal in a blue shirt, scored against West Ham in May, 1986

MESMERISED:
Gary Stevens watches as Coventry City's Steve Ogrizovic is beaten by this Graeme Sharp effort in August, 1985

NET RETURN: Another Sheedy celebration after his equaliser against Chelsea, March, 1986

SPOT OF BOTHER: Graeme Sharp fires wide from the spot against Chelsea in October, 1985. This was a game in which Neville Southall was sent off, forcing skipper Kevin Ratcliffe to go in goal

INCHY AT THE DOUBLE: Wearing the famous number nine for once, Adrian Heath scores one of two against West Brom at Goodison Park in August, 1985. This came after a long injury lay-off

MAN IN THE MIDDLE:
Alan Harper in action against Birmingham at St. Andrew's in January, 1986

UNSTOPPABLE: Graeme Sharp scores the only goal of the game against Ipswich at Goodison in April, 1986. Paul Cooper is left helpless

175

A FAMILY AFFAIR:
Young fans and old
applaude Adrian Heath as
one young boy peeps
through the old fences
that became a blight on
football grounds all over
the country

**THE BLACK HORSE
CUP FINAL:**
When your team has
galloped home at
Wembley, you need a
special vantage point
to pay your respects

HEATH IN FULL FLIGHT: Adrian took some stopping

JUMP FOR JOY: It's Gary Lineker
at Goodison Park

**ROYAL BLUE
ELATION:**
The Eighties
were just full
of joy

DEADLY DEREK: That's Mountfield in typical action, trying to reduce the arrears against QPR in September, 1985

ARISE SIR GARY: The fans salute a royal Blue knight as Lineker celebrates one of three against Birmingham in August, 1985

**SHEEDY'S A
SHARP-SHOOTER:**
Kevin drills
one in against
Manchester United in
December, 1985

MAKING HIS POINT: Neil Pointon
takes to the air to drill in a
spectacular shot in a 2-0 home win
over Villa in March, 1986

STRETCHING CHELSEA: Goodison action in March, 1986

SHARP TURN: Graeme uses his skill against Oxford

SPOT THE BALL: Don't worry, boys. It's in Nev's safe hands at Loftus Road

ACROBATIC: Gary Lineker scores against Coventry at Highfield Road in December, 1985

DON'T PANIC: A close call for Coventry's
Steve Ogrizovic at Goodison with Gary
Lineker in close attendance

WHERE'S SHARPY?: That's Reidy closing in on the box against Spurs in February, 1986. He later scored the only goal of the game as he marked his return after a five month absence

WANG, BANG, WALLOP:
Don't mess with Pat Van
den Hauwe. Action against
Oxford United

HORIZONTAL HIT MAN: Graeme Sharp scores Everton's
third and his second in the 3-1 win over Manchester United

SUPER OPENER: Graeme Sharp nets in the 2-0 October, 1985 win over Oxford

DOMINANT IN EVERY SITUATION: The very special Peter Reid against Manchester United during a goalless draw on Easter Monday, 1986.

JUST WIDE: Paul Bracewell lets fly against West Brom in August, 1985

STEP ASIDE:
Gary Lineker in the
fray against Queens
Park Rangers

PUT IT THERE: The job has been done and Gary Stevens shakes on it

OVER THE LINE: Villa keeper Nigel Spink looks up, relieved that he is on the right side of the post with the ball in his hands after this battle with Graeme Sharp

10, 8, 6 . . .

Where's the 4 to complete the sequence? Bracewell, Lineker and Reid can't wait
for the skipper after Peter scored the winner against Spurs in February, 1986

SUPER SAVE: Nottingham Forest's Steve Sutton denies the diving Gary Lineker in November, 1985

NOT QUITE: Peter Reid shoots against Birmingham at the start of the 1985/86 season. David Seaman saves

86/87
Yet another title

IN MANY RESPECTS, THIS WOULD BE THE CAMPAIGN THAT WOULD SINGLE MANAGER HOWARD KENDALL OUT AS A SHREWD TACTICIAN AND A CANNY JUDGE OF WHAT WAS BEST FOR THE WIDER GOOD OF HIS TEAM.
 HAVING SACRIFICED ONE OF THE MOST PROLIFIC GOALSCORERS IN THE WORLD GAME, EVERTON HAD THE TRIED AND TRUSTED PARTNERSHIP OF MESSRS SHARP AND HEATH BACK IN TANDEM AS A NEW SEASON KICKED OFF AT HOME TO NOTTINGHAM FOREST. WOULD GARY LINEKER BE MISSED OR WOULD KENDALL'S LOGIC BE PROVED RIGHT?

There was an early sign when the matchwinner on day one was not a striker, but a midfielder with probably the best left foot in the game. Kevin Sheedy's double saw off Nottingham Forest.
 Kendall had not intended to make a major signing in the summer, but injury fears over centre-half Derek Mountfield had inspired a swoop for Norwich City captain Dave Watson whose £900,000 fee was substantial for a defender at that time.
 Some fans were shocked when the manager then picked up a full-back who was in the twilight of his career, having spent 15 years at Manchester City. Paul Power cost just £65,000, but his impact was

to be truly remarkable for a 32 year old who suddenly found himself helping to inspire another powerful title push by the Mersey Blues.

Kendall had also sought cover with the acquisition of midfielder Kevin Langley from Wigan, a player who had looked very comfortable on the ball at a lower level and who suddenly found himself thrust into top flight action with the massively influential Peter Reid out for what turned out to be an agonising five month spell on the sidelines, during which time he managed one substitute appearance.

Everton won just four of their opening ten games, hardly Championship form. Watson was taking his time to settle and the fans were beginning to ask one or two questions going into the November.

Mountfield reappeared on the scene with injury worries still hanging over him. Watson would sit out six games, but Messrs Kendall and Harvey had tremendous confidence in him and decided that a timely moment for reinstatement would be when his old club Norwich visited Goodison on December 6. The Blues would romp home 4-0 thanks to Heath, Power, Pointon and Steven. Significantly, Watson had a fine game and he would never look back.

With the fans now recognising his character and rock-solid ability as a stopper, the big defender went from strength to strength. Kendall, looking to increase his attacking options in a season that was dogged by injury, signed Wayne Clarke from Birmingham. It would be an astute addition at a key time. Probably even more important was the capture of a classy, mobile and supremely confident midfielder from Leeds United, Ian Snodin.

What made the deal extra special for all Evertonians was the fact that the player turned his back on a move to Kenny Dalglish's Liverpool to complete an £840,000 move to Goodison. The versatile Snodin would prove his quality as a defender as well as a midfielder and his confidence rubbed off on all around him.

One of the real stars of this campaign was the supremely skilful Trevor Steven whose 14 goals from 41 appearances made him top scorer. Another midfielder, the equally brilliant Kevin Sheedy, weighed in with 13 from just 28 games. Heath got his usual solid return of 11, but this was not a season dominated by any one individual. Wayne Clarke's five goal input late on, including a treble against Newcastle, was also important.

Neville Southall came back from a terrible injury to reclaim his undisputed place as Everton's number one. Kendall's belief in the team against the superstar individual paid off handsomely as the Blues clinched the title three games out, fittingly as Watson returned to Norwich.

The explosive winner came from another unexpected source, full-back Pat Van den Hauwe. To confirm their superiority at the top, Everton finished in style with a home double against Luton and Tottenham.

It was somewhat fitting that Derek Mountfield came off the bench to score the final goal on the final day of that eventful season. He had been a real fans' hero, but had been forced to watch much of the action from the sidelines, both through injury and the great form of Watson. But Derek had played his part in the previous four years and it was right that he was out there on the pitch as the fans celebrated their second Championship in three years.

Incredibly, the glory that had been the mid-Eighties would soon fade. Howard Kendall, Manager of the Year once more and the mastermind with Colin Harvey of a real golden era would make a shock decision to leave the Blues and link up with Athletic Bilbao in Spain.

Everton would finish fourth, eighth, sixth, ninth, twelfth and then thirteenth in subsequent seasons as the memories of skipper Kevin Ratcliffe holding aloft one trophy after another began to fade.

Even worse would follow after an all too brief interlude during which Joe Royle brought further FA Cup glory to Goodison.

The Eighties years remain an indelible episode in Everton's rich history. It was the age of the magnificent Z-Stars . . .

UNITED TAMED:
Kevin Sheedy
crashes home
Everton's second in
the 3-1 win over
Manchester United in
September, 1986

The Match...

MAGIC THAT ATKINSON JUST COULD NOT BUY!

EVERTON 3 MANCHESTER UNITED 1
League. September 21, 1986

Everton (4-4-2): Mimms, Mountfield, Ratcliffe, Watson, Power, Steven, Langley, Heath, Sheedy (Adams 80), Sharp, Wilkinson.
Manchester United (4-4-2): Turner, Sivebaek, Albiston, Whiteside (Olsen 75), McGrath, Moran, Robson, Strachan, Stapleton, Davenport, Moses.
Referee: Mr. J. B. Worrall.
Goals: Sharp (6 mins) 1-0. Robson (15) 1-1. Sheedy (45) 2-1. Heath (89) 3-1.
Attendance: 25,845.

By Ken Rogers

THE stars Ron Atkinson could not buy increased his personal misery at Goodison Park yesterday.

Graeme Sharp and Kevin Sheedy - two men the Manchester United boss had eyed with particular envy in recent seasons - set Everton on their way to a battling 3-1 victory which captured the imagination of a nationwide television audience.

In between, England skipper Bryan Robson conjured up an effort which kept his side in the hunt until the final minute when Adrian Heath turned the screw with his first goal of the season.

The points hoisted the Blues into second place in the table behind Nottingham Forest, but the simple fact that goalkeeper Bobby Mimms was a fourth Goodison hero reflects the end-to-end nature of an outstanding game.

United played their part, particularly in the second half when the brilliant Mimms left dead-ball expert John Sivebaek and striker Frank Stapleton totally stunned with outstanding saves.

United's determination and resolve throughout emphasised that talk of a crisis is more than a little premature.

But at the end of the day, the Blues had demonstrated yet again that they have got something of an Indian sign over Atkinson and his men in the League. The fans left Goodison talking about three of the best goals you will see on any ground this season.

The game was also memorable for a number of fascinating individual battles. Paul Power had an outstanding game at left-back in what was a very personal 'derby' encounter. The former Manchester City defender faced the old enemy with pride and confidence, using his vast experience to good effect against the lively, powerful, attacking runs of Gordon Strachan.

Power had the bonus of laying on the opening goal, his perfectly struck cross from the left being met majestically by Sharp who rose above Kevin Moran after six minutes like some latter-day Dixie Dean to send a glorious header into the net off the underside of the bar.

The description is rather apt in the week when the name of the late, great Dixie will be back in the news.

Tomorrow the Echo will name the latest recipient of the Dean Memorial Trophy, an occasion which always generates vivid memories of yesteryear and the scoring exploits of the man who still holds the League scoring record with 60 goals.

He would have been proud of Sharp's classic header after six minutes which provided the Blues with a dream start.

To their credit the visitors powered back. Robson drove through a ruck of players after Kevin Ratcliffe only half cleared a Strachan corner. Heath replied with a header that went narrowly wide after Sheedy and Kevin Langley had combined on the flank.

Sheedy had better luck as the half drifted into injury time, demonstrating that he HAS got a right foot, by lashing Everton back in front with his fifth goal of the season.

It was a hectic, fiercely competitive encounter. You do not expect anything less when Merseyside confronts Manchester. The little cameos that unfolded included an epic confrontation between Sharp and Kevin Moran. The Irishman climbed all over his rival at times, but Sharp gave as good as he got.

Derek Mountfield continues to prove that there is life for him after Dave Watson, producing an enthusiastic and determined display at right-back where injuries to Gary Stevens and Alan Harper threatened to leave a gaping hole.

Adrian Heath looked better for a midfield challenge, Howard Kendall using Paul Wilkinson as a hard-running foil for Sharp and playing Heath behind them. He earned his reward in the 89th minute in memorable fashion. Sharp out-headed Moran on the halfway line. Langley showed a cool head to hold the ball up on the right and when the low cross finally came in, Heath dived forward to glance a header beyond Turner.

He had waited nearly 630 minutes for his first League goal of the season, but what a way to get off the mark. And what a way to finish an excellent match which left Everton as the only unbeaten team in the top flight.

Everton had excellent man-of-the-match contenders throughout their ranks.

Graeme Sharp's reward for a battling performance was a spectacular headed goal. Derek Mountfield did an excellent job at right-back and when United did get through, Bobby Mimms was in inspirational mood.

But the verdict went to Paul Power on a day when he revelled in the challenge against the old enemy. He put quality crosses in every time he overlapped down the left and defended well against one of United's best performers, the busy Gordon Strachan.

HOWARD KENDALL
– inside the dressing room

Here we were, emphatically beating Manchester United early in the 1986/87 season with a team that was fundamentally different to the one that won us the 1985 title. Dave Watson had been signed because of the doubts about Derek Mountfield's fitness. Paul Power was perhaps a more surprising acquisition, but I rated him highly. We even had Kevin Langley in midfield, captured from Wigan after a swoop into the lower divisions. Paul Wilkinson would ultimately provide cover up front.

Injuries were an issue for us and we used a lot of players during what would be another highly successful Championship year. Of course, one major enforced change had to be made between the posts where we were now looking to Bobby Mimms to prove he could produce the goods in the top flight.

We had lost the highly influential Neville Southall the previous season, the day before the transfer deadline. Nev suffered a terrible injury playing for Wales. That was when I went down to London to try and influence Tottenham's vastly experienced keeper Pat Jennings to sign as cover for Bobby.

It inspired a quiz question that still foxes people all over the country about Pat's list of clubs.

All managers know that you will never win a major trophy without a top class keeper. Bobby Mimms did really well for us in Neville's absence and played enough games in that 1986/87 season to earn a title medal, although we all knew that it was just a matter of time before Nev would return.

When we beat Man United in that September encounter in 1986 there was a genuine feeling of optimism that we could secure our second Championship crown, having just missed out the year before to Liverpool. United had title hopes of their own, but Sharp, Sheedy and Heath produced the goals that overshadowed them.

I was interested to note that the Echo man-of-the-match on the Monday went to Paul Power. A few eyebrows had been raised when I signed him from Manchester City, notably because of his age, but I knew what a great professional he was.

This was actually demonstrated when we met his old club that season at Maine Road.

This had been his spiritual home in a way and he actually scored. Paul didn't make a big song and dance about it. He just turned away and I think the home fans respected that.

Everyone remembers when Denis Law left Manchester United to sign for City. He scored in a subsequent Manchester derby and dispensed with his famous cocky hand in the air salute. He couldn't bring himself to rub United's noses in it.

It's what you expect from good professionals and Paul was certainly one of those. I was certainly delighted to have him.

MR VERSATILE:
Alan Harper in full
flight. He proved a
great buy for Howard
Kendall and scored a
crucial goal at
Stamford Bridge

The Match...

HARPER IS TOP OF THE POPS

CHELSEA 1 EVERTON 2
League, April 4, 1987

Chelsea (4-4-2): Godden, Clarke, McLoughlin, Pates, Dublin, Nevin, Wood, Hazard, Jones, Durie, Dixon. Sub: West.
Everton (4-4-2): Southall, Stevens, Watson, Ratcliffe, Power, Steven, Reid, Harper, Sheedy (Pointon 79 mins.), Clarke, Heath.
Referee: Mr. T Holbrook.
Goals: McLoughlin (23 o.g.) 0-1; Dixon (72) 1-1; Harper (77) 1-2.
Bookings: McLoughlin (foul), Sheedy (foul).
Attendance: 21,914.

By Ric George

HOWARD KENDALL must have taken an extra long look at the Sunday papers and savoured the sight of Everton proudly sitting on top of Division One.

Having played one game less than rivals Liverpool, the Blues manager knows that after winning a tricky fixture at Chelsea, the destiny of the League Championship is once again in the hands - or at the feet - of his impressive squad.

With the Reds pre-occupied with their quest for Littlewoods Cup honours, Everton knew they had to return from Stamford Bridge with three points to top the table and press further their claims for a title which had seemed beyond them only weeks ago.

Two successive wins in the capital is a fine achievement and the Blues deserve full credit for recovering from the blow of conceding an equaliser to claim victory with a stunning goal.

Mr. Versatility, Alan Harper, doubled once more as Mr. Reliability when, 13 minutes from time, he struck a superb right foot shot to leave Tony Godden wishing he was six inches taller.

Picking up the ball from Peter Reid, Harper - in for the suspended Ian Snodin - looked up and saw his drive from 25 yards whizz over the head of the diminutive keeper.

A minute later he sent another effort thundering against the bar, demonstrating the confidence acquired from his golden strike.

It was fitting that Harper should have the last say, having been subjected to the chants, "Let him die", from the home crowd, after McLoughlin's wicked challenge had left him writhing.

But while the former Anfield reserve justifiably makes the headlines, Neville Southall's contribution should not go unnoticed.

Undisputed hero at Arsenal last week, the Welsh international, although not given as much work this time, again came to the rescue when danger loomed.

Indeed he produced a save of the highest class, palming away Dixon's header when the scores were level. Had that effort found the net, it is hard to imagine Harper producing his special seconds later.

Southall's stop was the turning point of the match which really sprang to life in the second half.

The Blues had taken a 23rd minute lead when, under pressure from the impressive Dave Watson, McLaughlin clinically despatched Harper's corner into his own net.

Chelsea, with Hazard and particularly Nevin looking dangerous, played some surprisingly neat stuff after the break. And their toil was rewarded when Dixon raced on to Wood's pass to fire them level.

Barracked by the Chelsea fans, the plodding Kerry Dixon had been looking more like his namesake from Dock Green than an international striker, and needed the goal if only to boost his own confidence. That it certainly did, and with 18 minutes remaining Chelsea scented victory.

But Southall and Harper killed their hopes to push Everton into a league position they aim to maintain.

Gary Stevens, Kevin Ratcliffe, Alan Harper and Peter Reid were all worthy contenders for the man-of-the-match award.

The defenders held firm and broke when they could, while the midfield men were constantly prompting and winning tackles. But the vote goes to Dave Watson, who produced a solid display at the back and caused problems when he went forward and made some timely interceptions and clearances.

HOWARD KENDALL
– inside the dressing room

This victory at Chelsea in the title run-in meant that the destiny of the Championship was back in our hands. It was the reverse of the previous year when a defeat at Oxford had handed the initiative to our nearest rivals Liverpool.

It was a magnificent achievement to be in the driving seat because of the number of players we had been forced to use. Alan Harper scored our winner and I was delighted. Many saw him as a utility player and not an automatic first choice, but he played a tremendous amount of games and I rated him highly. His technique was good and he was also very adaptable.

Alan was a local lad who had a lot of confidence in his own ability. It was not mis-placed. He was a great example to kids in how to control a ball.

He wasn't looked on as one of the big stars, but he certainly had my respect.

Dave Watson got the man-of-the-match verdict at Stamford Bridge. You don't want your goalkeeper to be star man, but you don't mind when the verdict goes to one of those in front of him because it means the opposition are not getting through. Dave was our rock. Full credit to him for the way he established himself in that title-winning year.

We signed him from Norwich, but he had also been on Liverpool's books. He also replaced a Goodison fans' favourite in Derek Mountfield and so he had a tough challenge ahead of him in that 1986/87 campaign. It took a little while for him to settle and produce the form we knew he was capable of, but then it had taken Gary Lineker until Christmas to get into his stride the previous year.

Dave came good in a massive way. His £900,000 fee was a lot of money at that time for a defender, but he was worth every penny and more. Few players have given such sterling service to Everton. He later became a great captain and held aloft the FA Cup. He even had a spell as caretaker manager. I was proud that my belief in him came off in a big way.

RED HAZE:
Neil McDonald is
dismissed as
Newcastle lose
their composure
at Goodison in
April, 1987.
Ironically, Neil
would later
become an
Everton player

The Match...

WAYNE'S WORLD AS TREBLE STUNS GEORDIES

EVERTON 3 NEWCASTLE UNITED 0
League, April 20, 1987

Everton: Southall, Stevens, Pointon, Ratcliffe, Watson, Harper, Steven, Heath, Clarke, Snodin, Power.
Newcastle United: M. Thomas, McDonald, P. Jackson, Roeder, Tinnion, Stephenson, (Steward 67), Gascoigne, Wharton, D. Jackson, Goddard, A. Thomas.
Referee: Mr K. Baker (Northants).
Goals: Clarke (49, 82, 90) 3-0.
Booking: Gascoigne (foul).
Sending off: McDonald (dissent).
Attendance: 43, 376.

By Ken Rogers

EVERTON strikers old and new were hailed in a carnival atmosphere at Goodison Park yesterday as Howard Kendall's side took a giant step towards claiming the title. First, Blues' reject Peter Davenport, who played for the 'A' team as an amateur and was released by Gordon Lee, was the toast of one half of Merseyside as news filtered through that the Manchester United forward had struck late against Liverpool. Then, only two minutes later, the Goodison crowd rose to acclaim Wayne Clarke's first ever hat-trick that widened the gap at the top of the table.

It has been a happy Easter for Everton and although no one at the club is talking prematurely about winning the League, they cannot escape the fact that victory in Saturday's Anfield derby will, in reality, earn them the Championship.

The Geordies had travelled to Merseyside in their masses, hoping to see their beloved Magpies chalk up their 10th match without defeat in a run that has taken them from last place to relative First Division safety. Throughout the match their chants echoed round the ground and it was shuddering to think how many more would have made the journey if their team had been worthy of their fine support.

Without producing their slickest performance of the season, the Blues spent the first half struggling to find a way through a stubborn United rearguard. Martin Thomas was responsible for keeping the score down, punching and parrying from Adrian Heath, clutching an Ian Snodin shot and turning aside Alan Harper's angled drive.

At the other end, Snodin was in the right place to clear Darren Jackson's effort off the line. But this, and two Andy Thomas shots that Neville Southall dealt with comfortably, was all the Newcastle attack had to offer.

However, inspired by Paul Gascoigne, the Geordies frustrated Everton and were always capable of sneaking a goal on the break. What a relief, therefore, when four minutes after the interval Wayne Clarke's header from Paul Power's clip found its way into the net off a post.

In fact, the former Birmingham striker could have opened his account much earlier when, from inside the six yard box, he somehow directed a header over. It certainly did not seem he would add to his tally when he failed to connect with a Kevin Ratcliffe free-kick after Peter Jackson had allowed him to stray in front of keeper Thomas.

But it all turned out right in the end, for eight minutes from time Heath raced onto Harper's pass before drawing Thomas and squaring for Clarke who had time to place his shot.

Then in injury time Wayne rose at the far post to nod in Power's cross and claim the matchball. Why Neil McDonald had to argue about the goal with so little time remaining and the result already decided, I know not. His subsequent sending-off didn't even give him the chance of taking an early bath.

Hunted afterwards by press and radio, Clarke knew he had done a good afternoon's work, even if Peter Davenport had contributed to the celebrations. And with Graeme Sharp itching to return to first team action, Clarke's hat-trick leaves Howard Kendall with what must be a delightful derby dilemma.

 STAR MAN

Wayne Clarke's hat-trick cannot go unnoticed and it looks like the latest Goodison signing has really settled in at his new club. As usual, Paul Power gave his best and created two goals with accurate crosses from both wings.

But it is Adrian Heath who wins the vote for his non-stop running and total effort, symbolised by the fine part he played in the second goal.

HOWARD KENDALL
– inside the dressing room

We were in unstoppable form as the 1986/87 season reached its climax. The 3-0 win over a Newcastle side that included a young Paul Gascoigne was particularly satisfying. It was a day when Wayne Clarke grabbed a hat-trick. It pleased me because it proved I was right to sign him. I knew that Wayne had good technique, but his body language sometimes suggested that he was a bit lazy and possibly couldn't care less. That certainly wasn't the case.

My view was that his control and technique meant that he could lead the line for us. Players like Adrian Heath would clearly be working very hard. You would instinctively look at him and say: "Yes, he's doing the business." With Clarkey, it wasn't so apparent, but you had to look at his intelligence in and around the penalty area.

I remember he pulled off for a back post header to score against Newcastle. It was typical of his style.

This was a day when you couldn't help but see the ability of one of the opposition, even in defeat. The young Gascoigne had great skill and was clearly an exciting new talent, but he kept coming across to the dug-out and moaning to his manager. I remember thinking to myself: "Just get on with it, lad."

Gazza had this great confidence, even then, and his ability was there for all to see. But my instinct was to grab him and say: "Be a good pro. Concentrate on the game."

Obviously, Paul hated to lose and we were well in control that day. He was a bit like Alan Ball in that way. When things were not going well, Bally always had to show the crowd or the bench that he wasn't happy. He would be remonstrating with one of his team-mates or the referee. Then he would run 30 yards to kick someone up in the air. People thought Bally cared more because of this type of thing, but we all cared. It's just that we showed it in different ways. It struck a chord as I watched the young Gascoigne, but let's be clear. Both were great players.

LINKS POWER:
Gary Lineker hammers in a shot against Newcastle

POWER DRIVE:
Paul Power was
one of Howard
Kendall's
shrewdest buys.
The former
Manchester City
star defied the age
barrier to come in
and play a major
part in the 1987
title winning
season.
Here he opens the
scoring in the 4-0
win over Norwich
in December, 1986

The Match...

VAN DEN HOWITZER

NORWICH CITY 0 EVERTON 1
League, May 4, 1987

Norwich City (4-4-2): Gunn, Brown, Spearing, Bruce, Phelan, Butterworth, Williams, Drinkell, Rosario, Biggins (Fox 59), Gordon.
Everton (4-4-2): Southall, Steven, Van den Hauwe, Ratcliffe, Watson, Reid, Steven, Heath, Sharp, Snodin, Power.
Sub: Harper.
Goal: Van den Hauwe (45 seconds) 0-1.
Referee: Mr J. Bray (Blackley).
Attendance: 23,489.

By Ken Rogers

SECONDS out . . . bring on the Champions!
Howard Kendall's magnificent Blues stormed to glory at Carrow Road in the time it takes to say "Pat Van den Hauwe's a striking genius!"

Having struggled for 90 minutes to turn the title screw against Manchester City, Everton took just 45 seconds to produce the goods against shell-shocked Norwich City.

A blockbuster of a shot, straight out of the Kevin Sheedy shooting manual, exploded from the right boot of a man who is more renowned for his ferocious tackling than his lethal finishing.

It wasn't so much Van den Hauwe as Van den Howitzer as the ball flew into the net like an Exocet Missile. It triggered off an ecstatic response from the 7,000 Evertonians who had made the long trek to East Anglia.

Their triumphant, deafening roar carried on the wind all the way to Merseyside.

The Canaries - looking for their highest ever position in the top flight - had indicated before the game that they were determined to spoil the party, but the dream start gave the Blues' defence an inner steel.

Dave Watson in particular was in commanding form, looking solid and confident against his old club. Skipper Kevin Ratcliffe was also an inspiration throughout and both Van den Hauwe and Gary Stevens showed their international class.

Everton's slender lead was only threatened twice when Kevin Drinkell and Robert Rosario missed out with first half headers.

At the Norwich end, Steve Bruce had to kick off the line from Trevor Steven as Everton became the first team to win TWO title trophies in the same season. They will collect the new "Today" award as well as the historic Championship silverware that has been kept under wraps in ludicrous fashion for three years at the whim of the previous sponsors.

The Blues have more than earned their title crown, surviving a traumatic season on the injury front that would have destroyed most clubs. Strength in depth has been Everton's password to glory. You could sense that it was going to be a royal blue day. It was as if the Gwladys Street had been transported lock, stock and barrel to Carrow Road. When they roared "Bring On The Champions" the players emerged into the sunshine with a single-minded resolve to bring the great race to a climax.

Everton secured a corner inside ten seconds that was played into the box by the evergreen Paul Power. Trevor Steven and Graeme Sharp both tried to cash in and when the ball finally fell to Van den Hauwe 15 yards out, his finishing was on a par with his tackling - devastating!

Nothing was held in reserve! Gary Lineker, for one, would have approved and there lies a tale. Everton's 72nd League strike of the season maintains their status as the First Division's leading scorers. This is despite selling the man whose goalscoring exploits were the talk of the whole world last summer.

Kendall - having decided to cash in on Lineker - firmly believed that the goals would come from a variety of sources instead of from one rich vein of talent. Van den Hauwe's Championship winner emphasised the point.

The Barcelona deal was a gamble, but how handsomely it has paid off. Everton's success, after missing out in agonising fashion last season, has been down to all-round teamwork and one man in particular, 33 year-old Paul Power, has been a crucial cog in the Championship machine.

I believe the PFA blundered badly when they failed to honour him as their Player of the Year. The sports writers' accolade always goes to the most effective, eye-catching performer and you can't argue with the choice of Clive Allen in that respect.

But the players' verdict has often been linked, not just with quality, but with outstanding professionalism, dedication and character. Power has had a fairytale year and he sums up perfectly the spirit of Everton '87.

Golden boots don't necessarily win you titles as the Blues found out at the death last season.

The key ingredient is balance. Howard Kendall has produced a vintage champagne blend and his reward must surely be the Manager of the Year award. Anything less would be an insult.

 STAR MAN

Everton's had outstanding man-of-the-match contenders in their defence. Pat Van den Hauwe's 45 second opener meant the Blues' rearguard had to concentrate for close on 90 minutes to keep the title on course. Skipper Kevin Ratcliffe was first class, but the verdict goes to Dave Watson who was solid as a rock against his old team .

HOWARD KENDALL
– inside the dressing room

When you think about the day when you might clinch a League Championship, you dream about a variety of different scenarios. Yes, it's great to win it at home in front of your own fans. That's special and it happened in 1970 and 1985. Some fans like the idea of clinching it with a victory over one of the other giants - a Manchester United or an Arsenal. For me, it doesn't matter how it happens or where the match is. Just to win a Championship proves you are the best and that's what is important. And so when our 1987 title opportunity opened up at Norwich, I was just deeply satisfied that we were in touching distance of another major success.

It was a day all Evertonians will remember along with all of the other glory days when silverware was won. I always smile when I think about the events of Carrow Road, and not just because our winning goal came from an unexpected source - Pat Van den Hauwe.

I was up in the Directors' Box when Pat scored. Naturally, I jumped up, and punched the air, watching the players and the fans celebrate in style. At Carrow Road, the seats flip straight back up when you get off them. I was so elated that I just didn't think. I sat back down again and ended up on the deck. At least it gave the home fans around me something to smile about.

Naturally, I wanted to be with my staff and close to the players on the final whistle and so I made my way down to the bench in the second half. By now the cameras were on me, waiting for the final whistle and the explosion of delight.

There were one or two anxious moments near the end and I jumped up again to shout to the lads. They had the same tip-up seats in the dug-out. Well, you can guess what happened. I sat down again, my eyes concentrating on the pitch. It was like one of those Christmas parties where someone pulls away the chair - and this time it was captured by the cameras.

Everyone on the bench laughed. I didn't care. I'd been smiling ever since Pat's effort hit the back of the net. Another title was in the bag.

I mentioned those different scenarios when you clinch some silverware. If it can't be at home then you want it to be as far away as possible so you can have a long and ecstatic celebration all the way back.

Norwich reminded me of Highbury in 1984 when we beat Southampton to reach the FA Cup final. That day I told the driver to take his foot off the gas and take the scenic route back. It was the same at Carrow Road, but this time it was even better. We were going back as the best.

The big frustration was that we were subsequently denied the opportunity to play in the European Cup and take the next step up the ladder because of the Heysel Stadium disaster. No one would want to underplay what happened when Italian fans were killed after that wall collapsed before the 1985 European Cup Final between Liverpool and Juventus. It was a real tragedy, but the subsequent UEFA ban was particularly severe because it punished clubs who were not involved. We were in the front line at Everton as the new Champions.

The rewards for teams in Europe, especially for the Champions, can be tremendous. It enables players and managers to test themselves at the next level. It often enables managers to bring in further star quality based on those financial rewards and the simple fact that you are playing in Europe. For fans, it takes them to exciting new places and brings world-class opposition into the picture.

For me, the biggest disappointment was the fact that I believed we were the best in Europe at that time. I felt we could have won the Champions Cup and that would have meant so much to me as a manager and to everyone connected with our great club.

1986/1987 ENGLISH DIVISION 1 TABLE

	P	HW	HD	HL	HGF	HGA	AW	AD	AL	AGF	AGA	PTS	GD
Everton	42	16	4	1	49	11	10	4	7	27	20	86	+45
Liverpool	42	15	3	3	43	16	8	5	8	29	26	77	+30
Tottenham	42	14	3	4	40	14	7	5	9	28	29	71	+25
Arsenal	42	12	5	4	31	12	8	5	8	27	23	70	+23
Norwich	42	9	10	2	27	20	8	7	6	26	31	68	+2
Wimbledon	42	11	5	5	32	22	8	4	9	25	28	66	+7
Luton	42	14	5	2	29	13	4	7	10	18	32	66	+2
Nottm Forest	42	12	8	1	36	14	6	3	12	28	37	65	+13
Watford	42	12	5	4	38	20	6	4	11	29	34	63	+13
Coventry	42	14	4	3	35	17	3	8	10	15	28	63	+5
Man Utd	42	13	3	5	38	18	1	11	9	14	27	56	+7
Southampton	42	11	5	5	44	24	3	5	13	25	44	52	+1
Sheff Wed	42	9	7	5	39	24	4	6	11	19	35	52	-1
Chelsea	42	8	6	7	30	30	5	7	9	23	34	52	-11
West Ham	42	10	4	7	33	28	4	6	11	19	39	52	-15
QPR	42	9	7	5	31	27	4	4	13	17	37	50	-16
Newcastle	42	10	4	7	33	29	2	7	12	14	36	47	-18
Oxford	42	8	8	5	30	25	3	5	13	14	44	46	-25
Charlton	42	7	7	7	26	22	4	4	13	19	33	44	-10
Leicester	42	9	7	5	39	24	2	2	17	15	52	42	-22
Man City	42	8	6	7	28	24	0	9	12	8	33	39	-21
Aston Villa	42	7	7	7	25	25	1	5	15	20	54	36	-34

1986/87 LEAGUE STATS:

Home games in bold

AUG					
23	**Nottm Forest**	W 2-0	Sheedy 2		35,198
25	Sheff Wed	D 2-2	Langley, Sharp		33,007
30	Coventry	D 1-1	Marshall		13,504
SEP					
2	Oxford Utd	W 3-1	Harper, Langley, Steven (pen)		26,018
6	**QPR**	D 0-0			30,173
13	Wimbledon	W 2-1	Sheedy, Sharp		11,708
21	**Man Utd**	W 3-1	Heath, Sheedy, Sharp		25,843
27	Tottenham	L 0-2			28,007
OCT					
4	**Arsenal**	L 0-1			30,007
11	Charlton	L 2-3	Sheedy 2		10,564
18	Southampton	W 2-0	Steven (pen), Wilkinson		18,009
25	**Watford**	W 3-2	Mountfield 2, Steven (pen)		28,577
NOV					
2	West Ham	L 0-1			19,094
8	**Chelsea**	D 2-2	Steven (pen), Sheedy		29,727
15	Leicester	W 2-0	Heath, Sheedy		13,450
23	**Liverpool**	D 0-0			48,247
29	Man City	W 3-1	Heath 2, Power		27,097
DEC					
6	**Norwich**	W 4-0	Heath, Power, Pointon, Steven (pen)		26,746
13	Luton	L 0-1			11,151
20	**Wimbledon**	W 3-0	Heath, Sheedy, Steven		25,553
26	Newcastle	W 4-0	Heath, Steven 2, Power		35,079
28	**Leicester**	W 5-1	Heath 2, Sheedy, Wilkinson, Opp own-goal		39,730
JAN					
1	Aston Villa	W 3-0	Harper, Steven, Sheedy		40,203
3	QPR	W 1-0	Sharp		19,287
17	**Sheff Wed**	W 2-0	Steven (pen), Watson		33,011
25	Nottm Forest	L 0-1			17,009
FEB					
7	Coventry	W 3-1	Heath, Steven (pen), Stevens		30,402
14	Oxford Utd	D 1-1	Wilkinson		11,878
28	Man Utd	D 0-0			47,421
MAR					
8	Watford	L 1-2	Heath		14,014
14	Southampton	W 3-0	Opp own-goal, Power, Watson		26,564
21	Charlton	W 2-1	Steven (pen), Stevens		27,291
28	Arsenal	W 1-0	Clarke		36,218
APR					
4	Chelsea	W 2-1	Harper, Opp own-goal		21,914
11	**West Ham**	W 4-0	Clarke, Reid, Stevens, Watson		35,731
18	Aston Villa	W 1-0	Sheedy		31,218
20	**Newcastle**	W 3-0	Clarke 3		43,576
25	Liverpool	L 1-3	Sheedy		44,827
MAY					
2	**Man City**	D 0-0			37,541
4	Norwich	W 1-0	Van den Houwe		23,489
9	Luton	W 3-1	Sharp, Steven 2 (pens)		44,092
11	Tottenham	W 1-0	Mountfield		28,287

Final League Position: 1st in Division One

STEP ASIDE: Peter Reid steps in against Watford in March, 1987 with a typically robust challenge

ALL SQUARE: Graeme Sharp equalises to make it 1-1 at Shefield Wednesday in August, 1986. The game finished 2-2

SANDWICHED:
Paul Wilkinson is blocked out by Nottingham Forest's Ian Bowyer and Chris Fairclough in January, 1987

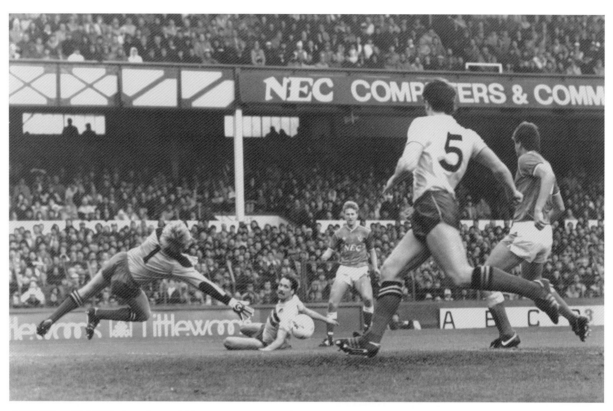

ACTION STATIONS: Everton put the pressure on Watford in October, 1986

GIVE US A CHEER: Graeme Sharp's mazy run and dribble resulted in the only goal against Queens Park Rangers in January, 1987

WHAT A GOAL: Adrian Heath is congratulated after scoring against Watford in March, 1987

BALLET POSE: It's Sharp and Heath, the song and dance men after Graeme's winner against Wimbledon at Plough Lane in September, 1986. The final score was 2-1 to the Blues

FIVE ALIVE: Another Derek Mountfield strike at Goodison, another moment to celebrate in style. The opponents were Watford and the Blues won 3-2 in October, 1986. Derek actually grabbed a double, scored an own goal and also conceded a penalty!

LONDONERS HAMMERED: Adrian Heath piles on the pressure in a 4-0 win over West Ham in April, 1987

SKY BLUES TAMED: Adrian Heath celebrates after scoring in the 3-1 win over Coventry City in February, 1987

ON THE ATTACK:
It's Dave Watson in action against Queens Park Rangers in January, 1987. The man trying to close him down is Sammy Lee, better known as a committed Red

PERFECT PAUL:
Ian Snodin and Adrian Heath look pleased,
but the goal hero was Paul Power against
Southampton in March, 1987

WRONG WAY KEEPER, RIGHT WAY TREVOR: Steven's spot-kick masterclass. The opponents were Norwich City and the Bllues won the game 4-0 in December, 1986. Trevor scored ten pens that season!

FLYING HIGH: Ian Snodin's first goal for Everton, scored at Bradford in the fourth round of the FA Cup in January, 1987

JUST BRILLIANT: Adrian Heath celebrates scoring one of the finest goals ever seen at Goodison, during the 4-0 win over Norwich City in December, 1986. It was a right foot volley following a delicate chip by Kevin Sheedy over the defence. Those shorts were a real fashion statement!

PAT STOOPS TO CONQUER: It's Van den Hauwe getting in a header against Manchester United. This Old Trafford affair actually finished goalless in February, 1987

SPOT THE BALL: Paul Wilkinson concentrates on putting off the keeper in the 1-1 draw at Oxford in February, 1987

OH SO HAPPY: Adrian Heath after opening the scoring in Everton's 3-1 win at Manchester City in November, 1986

SKY BLUE, HIGH BLUE: Coventry's Steve Ogrizovic clears from Graeme Sharp in the 1-1 draw at Highfield Road in August, 1986

I GET KNOCKED DOWN, BUT I GET UP AGAIN: Adrian Heath will soon be back in the action after clashing with Watford goalkeeper Steve Sherwood in the 3-2 victory in October, 1986

STYLE, POISE AND POWER: Adrian Heath's sensational goal against Norwich in December, 1986

PARTNERS IN HUGS:
Adrian Heath celebrates
Wayne Clarke's hat-trick
during the crucial win
over Newcastle in April,
1987

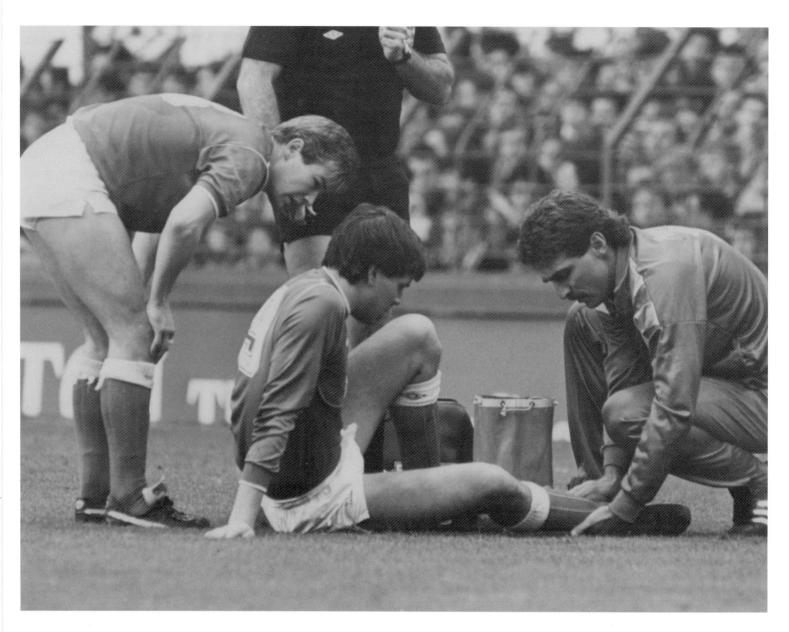

OKAY PAL? Adrian Heath shows concern for his injured partner Graeme Sharp as physio John Clinkard deals with the ankle problem

GO FOR IT, DEREK:
Mountfield in action
against Arsenal at
Goodison in October,
1986. It turned out to
be Everton's only loss
in the league at
home in 1986/87

SUPER WINNER: Alan Harper (hidden) lashes home the memorable winner at Chelsea in April, 1987. That's Pat Nevin trying to block

THE PROVIDER: Paul Power's cross leads to Wayne Clarke's opener against Newcastle United at Goodison Park in April, 1987. **Right:** A mean and moody Pat Van den Hauwe, no doubt dreaming about scoring an unexpected but sensational Championship winner at Norwich!

INSPIRATIONAL: Peter Reid in action in the 2-1 March, 1987 home win over Charlton

WILKO ELATION: Paul Wilkinson after scoring in the Littlewoods Cup against Sheffield Wednesday in October, 1986

SPOT ON: Trevor Steven puts Everton ahead with this penalty kick against Chelsea in November, 1986. It finished 2-2

DON'T WORRY: Inchy was the only one who got the ball, despite the Chelsea defender's best efforts in this clash in April, 1987

CHAMPIONS:
Steven and Stevens, but no mistaking the title delight

NOSE JOB: An unorthodox, but effective save by Nottingham Forest keeper Steve Sutton from this close range Trevor Steven effort in January, 1987

ON YER BIKE: A spectacular overhead kick from Adrian heath against Spurs. The 2-0 defeat was Everton's first in eight games in September, 1986

SHARP MOVE: Graeme opens the scoring in the 3-1 win
over Manchester United in September, 1986

VOLLEY GOOD EFFORT: Trevor Steven
connects in mid-air to highlight his skill,
watched by Nottingham Forest's Neil Webb

THE FACE OF GOODISON, 1987:
It was smiles all the way,
highlighted by Dave Watson and
Adrian Heath with the title looming.
Watson had just scored a great goal
against West Ham

TURNING AWAY: Trevor Steven leaves Wimbledon's Dave Beasant sprawling after 24 minutes of the 3-0 home win in December, 1986. Years later, it was described by rival chairman Sam Hamann as one of the best performances by any team against Wimbledon during their time in the top flight

STICKING TO YOUR MAN: Ian Snodin turns the tables on his rival from Solvite or Watford as they used to be known

TRICKY TREV: Steven gets in a shot against Oxford United in the 3-1 home win in September, 1986

HEAD BOY: Adrian Heath opens
Everton's account in the 2-0 win at
Leicester City in November, 1986.
Watching is a young Gary McAllister

ADRIAN'S BALL: He might have been small, but he could also walk tall. Heath leaps against Charlton

SPOT ON: Trevor Steven's accuracy leaves the Oxford keeper grasping fresh air. Everton won 3-1 in September, 1986

NEIL'S POINTER:
Neil Pointon scores his first goal for Everton, in the 4-0 win over Norwich City in December, 1986

EASY DOES IT: Graeme Sharp strokes in a shot with real accuracy to score against Manchster City in February, 1986

NEAR POST WINNER: Kevin Sheedy scored the only goal of the game at Villa Park on Easter Saturday, 1987, in front of a massive 15,000 Everton away fans! That is remarkable support in any situation

Howard's
A-Z Stars

NEVILLE SOUTHALL:

You find players in many different ways. Sometimes they impress when they play against you. Others come to your attention via the scouting system. Others have such outstanding talent that it speaks for themselves.

Occasionally, you pick up a gem via a highly unusual route. Such was the case with Neville Southall who, at his Everton peak, was the greatest goalkeeper in the world.

I had a friend, Norman Jones, who had hotels and one of these was in Llandudno. I was manager of Blackburn at the time where we had two goalkeepers, John Butcher and Jim Arnold.

Norman rang me and said: "You must come and see this young keeper who is playing for Winsford."

I wouldn't normally go myself to see a player at that level first time round, but I said: "Norman, for you I will come over,"

Norman's judgement was sound and I went back and asked the Blackburn chairman if I could sign him. The fee was £8,000. The answer was a straight: "No. You've already got two goalkeepers!"

Dave Connor, the ex-Manchester City player, was at Bury at the time and I had noticed him in the stands at the Winsford game. His club decided to meet the fee and so Neville went to Bury.

I was disappointed. You try to console yourself because it is so difficult assessing a goalkeeper. You can look over six or seven games and still be unsure. There will be games when they have little to do and other matches when they don't have to deal with too many crosses. You can't make an instant judgement, but I could see something in Neville.

My loss was Bury's gain. When I went to Everton in 1981, I felt there was a goalkeeping problem. I immediately went to Bury and asked them to name a price for Neville. In the end, he cost me £150,000, which was massively more than that £8,000 fee. But it would prove to be one of the best investments I ever made as a football manager.

I should add that I also had tremendous respect for Jim Arnold who had also proved himself at non-League level before stepping up into senior football. I signed Jim as well, but he was short term. Neville was the gem for the future, although Jim had cause to smile following a trip to Goodison by Bobby Robson who was the England manager.

Bobby came up to the boardroom after a game. He said: "I like your young Welsh goalkeeper. He played well today. I think he's got a chance."

Just one snag. It was Jim who was between the posts. We all laughed about it. I just looked on it as a tribute to BOTH of our keepers at that time.

I played in a few reserve team games when I came back to Everton. Nev was in goal. I thought to myself: "This is special."

When he eventually got into the first team, no one was going to touch him. But it all started with that phone call from a mate in Llandudno.

BOBBY MIMMS:

Bobby was an England Under 23 regular when I signed him from Rothertham as cover for Neville Southall. I was looking for a young keeper. I could see many good qualities and some possible weakness, but I knew he had real potential. You don't win international caps, even at that level, unless you've got talent.

Of course, I could not see him overtaking Neville, but then who could have ousted our Welsh international at that time? As it turned out, Bobby won an FA Cup Final medal and qualified for a Championship medal, proving himself after Neville suffered a terrible ankle injury playing for Wales.

In this respect, Bobby can look back with pride at his time at Goodison. I signed at least three keepers who didn't get a look-in with us. Pat Jennings didn't get further than wearing his Cup Final suit after agreeing to join us as cover for the 1986 Cup Final with Nev sidelined. Fred Barber and Alec Chamberlain were also talented reserves.

When you have got a Neville Southall, you have to think carefully when you are bringing someone in as an understudy. Do you sign a younger one or an older one? Usually it's easier with an older one who might be just happy to be at the club with an understanding that the number one is the number one. Bobby was a younger one and you instinctively expect them to get more frustrated and possibly ask for a move. As it turned out, he got his chance and took it.

It was pleasing because he had made some errors and I wondered if he could seriously fit the bill when Neville was injured. He came through in the end and proved me wrong.

JIM ARNOLD:

Jim's full-time football career started late. He was a part-timer with Stafford Rangers where he was capped at non-League level for England. When I went to Blackburn Rovers as player-manager, he was my first signing and I had no hesitation in signing him for Everton.

 He was a completely different character to Neville. Jim had arrived at Blackburn retaining some amateurish traits as a keeper, but he soon developed into a great pro. Martin Hodge and Jim McDonagh were at Everton when I arrived, but I felt the goalkeeping position was a priority to sort out and so I signed Neville and Jim. They got on well together and worked hard to help each other in training.

GARY STEVENS:

I always wanted pace at the back and with Gary Stevens, Kevin Ratcliffe and Pat Van den Hauwe we had that. Gary was a great athlete. He just ate up the ground when he got into his stride.

 When I first saw him, he was a young left-sided midfielder. I moved him to right-back and while it took him time to learn the position, he was soon excelling enough to be picked by England in that role.

Often you see defenders exposed by pacy forwards, but that was never the case with us at that time.

JOHN BAILEY:

What can I say about "The Bails?" He was a remarkable character. I always remember when I took over as player/manager of Blackburn Rovers. He was actually the first player ever to be transferred under what was then the new freedom of contract ruling. I didn't have any option when Everton came in for him.

 It went to a tribunal over the fee and, again, it was the first case judged in that way. They decided on £200,000 with another £100,000 after 50 games. These were difficult financial times for Blackburn. There was no Jack Walker ploughing in his millions at that time and so the money was welcomed by the club, even though I'd lost a talented full-back.

 We got the extra £100k in just 12 months, which says a lot about the impact he made at Goodison.

 I spoke to Gordon Lee at that time and he said: "I know Bails. He will excite the Goodison crowd, but I'm not sure away from home."

 John's qualities were clear and he never let us forget that he did something that the legendary Pele failed to do. Bails was always telling us that he scored from his own half in a game against Luton when the ball skidded over Jake Findlay. But we used to say: "Yes, but Pele meant to do it when he hit that famous shot in the 1970 World Cup that soared like a bird and had the goalkeeper scrambling back on his heels before the ball curved wide at the last moment!"

The one thing you could never take away from our left-back was that he could lift any dressing room with his humour. Who could forget the famous top hat he wore during the lap of honour after we beat Watford to win the FA Cup at Wembley? And don't ask me where he got those giant Elton John sunglasses!

That was typical John Bailey. He was magnificent to have around. We had some tremendous characters in our dressing room at that time and it makes it much easier for a manager, especially in tense situations when you want individuals to relax and go out and play the football you know they are capable of.

Mersey "derby" games always have people on edge, especially in the moments before the teams go out. I can remember the buzzer going to tell us to make our way into the tunnel. The lads began to line up and Bails shouted: "I've seen those Red Noses out there and I can't believe how nervous they are." He turned round to face the lads and had his shirt on back to front! It was typical of the kind of stunt he would pull to raise a laugh and boost the team morale. He was a one-off with his special brand of humour, but we had a number of great characters.

I remember when we were in Europe and the players' wages were linked with a crowd bonus if the gates topped 19,999. Sir Philip Carter used to come into the dressing room before games and go round the lads to wish them luck. Adrian Heath smiled and said to him: "I've had a look outside, Mr. Chairman, and the fans are queueing to get in. I expect the attendance is 19,999 again!" Everybody roared with laughter. It was typical banter from the lads.

PAT VAN DEN HAUWE:

I was at Birmingham when Pat signed in as a schoolboy. As Everton looked to strengthen further after the 1984 FA Cup Final, he immediately sprung to mind. I sent Terry Darracott down to Birmingham to watch him. He came back with a glowing report.

No disrespect to great left-footed left-backs like Ray Wilson and John Bailey, but I preferred a right-footer in that position. I thought they were better defenders because they were strong when people tried to come inside them. Of course, you want them to be able to go down the line and also show quality with the left foot in attacking positions. Terry had not seen that in Pat on that particular night because he rarely had the chance to get forward.

However, I felt that £90,000 was a good investment and we went ahead. I remember his debut well. It was at Arsenal and early in the game he got down the flank and whipped in a pearler of a cross. I turned to the lads in the dug-out and said: "That will do for me."

Some people had questioned the signing because Pat had been part of a "team within the team" at Birmingham, which included the likes of Mark Dennis. There had been reports about problems at the club and manager Ron Saunders decided to clear them out.

It would have been a problem if anyone had decided to sign two or three of them, but taking one away and putting him in a tremendous dressing room where they would soon be on top of him if there was an issue, I wasn't worried.

Having said that, they didn't call him "Psycho Pat" for nothing. It was just the way he reacted to a tackle or an incident on the pitch. He was not a dirty player. He was very steady on the field and a good tackler. Pat was also comfortable at centre-half.

As often happens, when you get a reputation it goes before you. Liverpool's Tommy Smith spent his last few years simply pointing the finger to threaten opponents. He'd been a hard man and done all that. Towards the end, his reputation was enough to give him an advantage.

Pat would glare at people. But he was actually a very good player and when we had a problem at centre-back he was our Player of the Season for me.

He had eligibility to play for Belgium through his father. Manager Guy Thys flew in to watch him in 1985. He was actually penciled in to play for their Under 21s against Spain. Suddenly there was press speculation that Pat might have to do national service in Belgium. I couldn't imagine him on a parade ground, doing drill.

Bobby Robson wanted him for England, but had strength at left-back. Not surprisingly, Kevin Ratcliffe and Neville Southall kept encouraging him to opt for Wales. He was a most unlikely "Welshman" with that strong London accent, but he chose that route to the international scene and it was a real coup for the Welsh.

I don't think Pat had a weakness on the field. He had pace, was strong and good in the air. He proved a great signing.

PAUL POWER:

Paul was a great professional. Because of his age, many wondered why I signed him from Manchester City, but his legs were still strong. He had always looked after himself and had captained City.

I approached City a few times and eventually persuaded them the time was right. They possibly thought they had seen the best of him, but I knew he still had a good engine and great experience. Sometimes you have to consider one or two of the older gems that are available.

Paul played 40 league games in that 1987 title-winning year, plus eight cup games. Not bad for a lad who was supposed to be past it.

KEVIN RATCLIFFE:

Kevin Ratcliffe had the honour of being Everton captain throughout the most successful period in the club's history, but when he was just a young left-back he could so easily have joined Blackburn Rovers. When I was player-manager at Ewood Park, Everton began to show an interest in the goalscoring Kevin Stonehouse.

 We asked Goodison chief scout Harry Cooke about a possible deal that would involve Ratcliffe, but then Everton's interest in Stonehouse cooled. They said they were not too sure about him, so I said okay.

 Ratters had been trying to establish himself in the Everton side, mainly at left-back, for a couple of seasons. He'd made two appearances in 1979/80, and then 20 the following year. This improved to 25 in my first season as manager, but I didn't feel left-back was his best position. Technically, he wasn't a cultured footballer, but I'll tell you what. In terms of pace and covering ability, he was tremendous.

 In 1982/83, with Billy Wright out of favour, Kevin began to form an excellent partnership with Mark Higgins. We started 1983/84 with Higgins and Derek Mountfield in the middle of the back four, but after just two games Kevin was back alongside Mark and that was only interrupted when Higgins' injury problems started to surface.

 This launched the new partnership of Ratcliffe and Mountfield and it proved tremendously successful. Rats was a great leader. That made my job easier in the dressing room. He was a strong character and you need that from your skipper. Kevin would hold aloft some famous silverware and played a significant part in that mid-Eighties success story.

MARK HIGGINS:

It's funny how something can happen that makes you re-think your logic on certain styles of play. In November, 1982 I had a problem with centre-back Billy Wright and disciplined him. He was left out for the away game at Ipswich and I was forced to play two left-sided centre-backs for the first time in Mark Higgins and Kevin Ratcliffe. As it turned out, they were superb together. Not many managers played with two left-siders. Generally, it was felt that the balance wasn't right.

 But we won that game 2-0 and retained the partnership for the remainder of the season. Mark became captain and was an important player for us going into that now momentous 1983/84 campaign, but he began to have problems in the pelvic area. Ironically, he found himself on the sidelines in the December and Kevin took on the skipper's mantle as we suddenly embarked on those two cup runs that would eventually make Wembley a very special place for us in 1984.

 When Rats held up the FA Cup, it must have been a painful experience for Mark. He would have been happy for his old partner, but cursing his luck that he was not the one leading the team up to the Royal Box.

That's football, I suppose. I still remember the day Mark Higgins joined Everton. I was still a player then. His father John had been a powerful defender with Bolton in the Fifties. I remember the young Mark arriving with his dad to sign. I immediately thought that here was a boy with the physique of a man. It meant he could jump ahead of some of his youth team colleagues into a more advanced stage during the late Seventies.

Mark had a little bit of deafness in one ear. When I became manager, I would be in the dug-out and Mark would come out of defence and play a great ball. I'd shout: "Well done lad" and he would clearly hear me above all the din and acknowledge it with real pride. Then he might play a bad ball and I would be up on my feet again, screaming: "What have you done?" It's funny, but he never heard me on those occasions! He'd blank me. Interesting, but the deafness seemed to be less apparent when he was playing well!

But then he was not the first. The great Alex Young had a hearing impediment. When he'd scored a couple at Goodison on the Saturday, he would be in the team meeting on the Monday and sitting up tall in his seat listening intently as Harry Catterick said: "Alex, you were superb. Great goals!"

Then we'd play away and Alex wouldn't be quite as impacting. Harry would be saying: "Alex, you were a disgrace," but the Golden Vision would be showing no reaction, having taken his hearing aid out! We'd be nudging him, saying: "The boss is talking to you."

Mark was a solid defender who had won a record 19 England schoolboy caps. It was a sad day when injury forced him to quit, although he would later make a surprise return to the game with Manchester United.

Looking back, I remember two images that appeared in the Liverpool Echo. One was a picture of Mark sitting in the Everton dressing room after we won the title in 1985. Obviously, he had been unable to play any part and you could see the sadness in his face. The picture showed Adrian Heath consoling him.

Then there was the final photograph on the day he finally left the club. He was walking across Goodison with his boots over his shoulder and carrying his young son who was looking back into the camera as Mark trudged away. It can be a tough game.

DEREK MOUNTFIELD:

It's difficult these days to go into the lower divisions and sign players who might make an early impact in the Premier League although it's still tempting for those managers who don't have too much money to spend. Back in the mid-Eighties you could still have a look and possibly take a chance. This is what happened with Derek Mountfield who had been impressing with Tranmere Rovers.

He was a local lad who desperately wanted to play for Everton. When we signed him, we didn't realise that here was a player who would not only defend solidly, but also provide a tremendous bonus in terms of goals scored at set-pieces.

Looking back, his return was fantastic. You buy them to be defenders first and foremost, but if they offer anything else it's a massive boost. John Hurst gave Harry Catterick that little bit extra when I was a player.

Derek came up with the goods more than once in 1984/85 when we won the League and Cup Winners Cup and very nearly made it an historic treble. I remember Derek scoring a crucial FA Cup sixth round equalising goal at Goodison as we drew 2-2 with Ipswich. Pat Van den Hauwe put in the cross and Derek got on the end of it.

As a manager, you enjoy things like that. Your left-back is the provider and your centre-back is the goalscorer. It shows that you don't just have to rely on the obvious sources. We went to Portman Road and Graeme Sharp got the winner to take us into the semis.

This time we faced Luton at Villa Park and Derek again produced the goods along with Kevin Sheedy to take us back to Wembley. The defeat in the Final against Manchester United was a blow, but fans will remember the excitement along the way and how Derek played his part.

He had a knee problem in 1985/86 and I wasn't sure whether he was going to be available for the start of the following season. I went out and bought Dave Watson from Norwich. Maybe Derek was disappointed with that, but when you are successful as a club, you must retain that success and centre-half is one of the most important positions in any team.

He can still look back on Championship and FA Cup glory and that is a wonderful thing for a local boy who was able to play for the team he always supported,

DAVE WATSON:

When I first contacted Norwich City to try and persuade their manager Ken Brown to sell their rock-solid defender, it was clear that he desperately didn't want to part with the lad. In fact, when the deal was done and Waggy had signed on the dotted line for £900,000, Brown said to me: "You've taken my right arm!"

He was clearly desolate at having lost his young skipper and I knew instinctively that I had a special player and a real leader. Dave took a little time to settle and his situation wasn't helped because the fans had really taken to Derek Mountfield who had not just been a powerful defender, but also a scorer of many key goals along the way.

But once Dave got into his stride, he would go from strength to strength.

I take pride in the fact that I signed a great professional who would give Everton magnificent service, both as a player, a captain who would eventually hold aloft the FA Cup himself, a coach and even a caretaker manager. He was a real leader and a no-nonsense player, the kind that helps you to sleep at night as a manager.

TREVOR STEVEN:

Trevor Steven developed into a magnificent right-sided midfielder for Everton although he took a little time to settle after stepping up a grade from Burnley. I always remember talking to Bob Paisley in the boardroom at Goodison. Liverpool were strongly linked with the lad before we signed him.

Bob said: "You were right about Steven." I said that I was surprised that we were the only ones left in for him in the final reckoning, despite all the rumours and reports. Bob said: "I looked at him and he never finished a game. That is why I didn't make a bid."

I'd also recognised that, but I knew that Trevor was very young and still learning to ride a tackle. He would be skipping past these big Second Division defenders. There would always come a time in the game when one of them would catch him and his slight frame meant he could not stand up to that.

I knew he would develop physically as well as further improving his game because he had so much skill. I took it as a real compliment when Bob Paisley praised my judgement.

Trevor had to learn, but when he found his feet at the top level he was one of the most outstanding players in the game.

PETER REID:

Peter Reid was tremendously influential in our mid-Eighties success story. You have to take into account that he was coming back from a devastating catalogue of injuries. He broke his left kneecap in 1978. He tore ligaments in his right leg in 1979. He had a cartilage operation in 1980 on his left knee. Then he broke his right leg in 1981.

It was against this backdrop of major problems that I signed him from Bolton in December, 1982 for £60,000. The fact that Gordon Lee had offered ten times that amount less than three years earlier did not alter the fact that it was something of a gamble.

It is to Peter's credit that he worked as hard as he did to become a magnificent player for Everton and England, but then he is a special character. He was simply more determined than most and had this tremendous will to win.

I felt we needed some character in the side at that time and hoped that he could put his injury nightmare behind him. As a manager, you need leaders on the pitch with experience. Peter and Andy Gray both came into this category, but they both came with risks because of the injuries they had suffered. Possibly I would not have been allowed to sign them today.

It was a big risk with both of them. Peter was an intelligent player who learned that he would have to approach his game in a different way because of his previous problems. He learned to actually intercept and anticipate rather than make a full-blooded block tackle. He was clever enough to still be a ball winner without having to make crunching challenges. He certainly didn't hold back in any situation, but he knew when and how to deal with opponents.

He would close people down without tackling and put people under pressure. If he was beaten, which was not very often, his mate Paul Bracewell was always behind him to finish off the job. They had a great understanding.

PAUL BRACEWELL:

I first came across Paul when I was at Stoke. I remember that the club did not have a youth policy and Alan Durban decided that we would use the summer to sort it out.

We spent the time looking at a number of recommended youngsters with a view to taking eight as apprentices out of a final list of about 15.

Brace was border line. By two votes to one, he became the eighth in the group. It's incredible how a player's whole life can hinge on such a decision. I watched him progress.

It was a compliment that when Alan Durban went to Sunderland, he took Paul with him. I couldn't say that he was a natural player. He simply worked very hard on his game to make himself a top class professional.

He didn't have the pace, but he developed a trick to give himself time in midfield, a change of direction and a dummy that allowed him to find time and space. He was an intelligent lad.

Most significantly, he was a workhorse who never shied away from anything. You talk about coaches helping people if they are prepared to listen. He is a perfect example of how you can develop an individual. He knew what you wanted from him and he formed that great partnership with Peter Reid, one of the best Everton have ever had in that area.

IAN SNODIN:

Ian Snodin came in at a timely moment to help us cement our title win in 1987. He was wanted by Liverpool's Kenny Dalglish. When we watched Ian prior to signing him, he was playing as sweeper.

He oozed quality and pace. It was a real battle with Liverpool to sign him from Leeds. I arranged a meeting at a hotel in Blackburn. He was due to see Kenny straight after.

He told me that he wanted to play centre-midfield. Liverpool initially wanted him to operate wide right, but said they would make him captain within 12 months.

I said: "Why don't you come to us now and play in your best position. Forget the captaincy. He thought about it and quickly decided not to see Kenny. Snods was a great player who was unlucky with injuries. If he had been able to retain his fitness, he would have been one of the best ever to play for England because of his pace, confidence and strength in the tackle.

KEVIN SHEEDY:

Kevin proved to be a tremendous signing for Everton. Whenever you reflect on key goals, it's amazing how often his name comes up as a provider or a finisher. He was very frustrated that he was not getting into the Liverpool side after joining them from Hereford. He was at the end of his contract and was not motivated to sign a new one, desperately wanting first team football.

I went to see him play in a reserve game at Preston with Colin Harvey. We were given permission to speak to him, but his demands were way in excess of what we were prepared to pay for someone who was not an established first teamer. After the talks I said to him: "We can't do it, Kev."

We went to Israel on an end of season tour, believing that to be the end of it. Then I suddenly received a phone call from chief scout Harry Cooke saying that Kevin had changed his mind and was prepared to accept the offer.

I said: "Leave it with me. I'll have a think about it today."

It wasn't an instant "yes" because he had not given us one, but I still knew he could do a good job for us. I finally got back to Harry and said: "Let him wait for the rest of the day before you get back. Then tell him we'll do the deal on our return."

I could have been headstrong because he had not initially leapt at the chance to join us. I could have said: "Forget it. You had your chance."

But we recognised his potential with that special left foot. He was an important piece in the jigsaw although he wasn't the best at warming up or exercising.

I remember one game when he was coming back from injury and was on the bench. During the game we had a problem on the left and I told "Sheeds" and Neil Pointon to warm-up. Neil was racing up and down like an Olympic sprinter. Kevin stood up, put his hands on his hips, and swayed gently from left to right. "Ready when you are," he said. I put him on. He kept his explosive moments for on the pitch when a lethal free-kick or a pinpoint cross would devastate the opposition.

ALAN HARPER AND KEVIN RICHARDSON:

Every successful team has to have its stars. But it also has to have its special professionals, lads who might not win the headlines week in, week out, but who play just as a big a part in the progress and success of a team. I had two in Alan Harper and Kevin Richardson.

Both might have been disappointed at times that they were not first choice, but the truth is that they would contribute up to 30 games which is a lot. Harper played 26 league games in that crucial 1983/84 season. Richo played in 27. Then there were the cups. I had to remind them of this at times.

Both knew how much I appreciated them as players and professionals, although I will never forget Richo's face the following season after he had scored twice and played tremendously well at Southampton. We then faced Spurs away with Kevin Sheedy declaring himself fit and ready for a recall.

I had to tell Richo I was leaving him out. We beat Tottenham 2-1 in front of 48,000 at White Hart Lane. I suppose the result vindicated me, but it was no consolation to Richo. As a manager, you have to make those kinds of decisions.

I know that deep down the lads recognised the respect I had for them. They were vital players. People talk about the Southalls, Reids and Grays and rightly so. At that time Kevin and Alan were not in my best eleven, but it's amazing how many games they played. Kevin Richardson won medals with us and then won a Championship medal with Arsenal to reinforce what a talented player he was. He also lifted the League Cup as captain of Aston Villa.

As for Harper, I actually signed him THREE times. I brought him from Anfield to Goodison. When I was at Manchester City, I signed him again from Sheffield Wednesday. Then I took him a third time, from Maine Road back to Goodison. That's quite a compliment and shows how highly I rated him.

ADRIAN HEATH:

I signed Adrian from Stoke for what was then an Everton club record of £700,000. It took him some time to settle. The move was a massive step for him. But it should also be remembered that I left Trevor Steven out early on after bringing him from Burnley. Young players, no matter how talented, have an adjustment to make when they step up a level. I always believed they had what it takes to be successful.

I had been at Stoke when Adrian was making his way through the ranks. He was a little pest to play against in training and I remembered that. He was always running past me and showing that infectious enthusiasm that was his hallmark. As a former cross-country champion, I also knew he had a tremendous engine.

I am a firm believer that any pairing up front must like and appreciate each other. It helps off the field and on it. If one partner is a lazy goal poacher and the other is doing all the work, it simply won't last.

Whoever played with Adrian Heath - whether it was Graeme Sharp, Andy Gray or both - they respected him. Likewise, he respected their input. There was trust and camaraderie amongst them. Our frontline was based around unselfish partnerships and the lads really appreciated each other.

If a manager can't get this relationship amongst his front men then he has got a problem.

The one thing Inchy might look back on is his failure to go on and win England caps. Possibly his goal ratio against appearances went against him at that level, but for Everton he was brilliant. It was a pleasure to manage him because of his skill and enthusiasm.

GRAEME SHARP:

Graeme must have been a nightmare to play against. He was very strong and had this knack of jumping early that frustrated centre-backs. He gained so many free-kicks as defenders tried to handle him in these situations. If a forward is up there as a defender tries to jump, the challenge always appears late and clumsy.

When you analysed Graeme as a player, it was difficult to criticise him or pick things out of his game. He was an excellent target man. Possibly he could have scored more tap-ins. A lot of his goals were spectacular efforts, like the famous strike at Anfield against Liverpool. Possibly he could have had a few more scruffy goals that are the mark of a successful centre-forward, but I'm not complaining. He played his part for us and his final goal tally for Everton was impressive. He scored 150 times in over 400 appearances.

ANDY GRAY:

There was a big risk attached to the signing of Andy Gray. We all knew what a great player he was, but his injury problems were well documented. I needed someone up there at that time who could lead the attack with power and confidence. What many people don't know is that I had the chance to bring Bob Latchford back to Everton on a free transfer. I respected Bob who was a superb striker. There were other options to Andy.

Ipswich Town's Paul Mariner was available for £600,000. Andy's fee of £280,000 reflected the risk, but in the end I decided to take it because I recognised the quality he could provide, backed up by his presence in the dressing room.

It turned out to be two years of absolutely magnificent service from the Scottish centre-forward. The first thing I had to do was stop him from training. All he wanted to do was bang the ball into the back of the net. It was important to be sensible when working him before games.

I remember speaking to our medical people on the day we signed him. They asked to see his appearance record for the two previous years. He'd actually managed about 30 games a season for Wolves. I was told that if he kept himself fit and worked on the quads to stabilise his knee, then there was no reason why he could not play at the highest level for at least another couple of years.

Andy was always very confident and I was keen to complete the deal to ensure he was available for our impending game at home to Nottingham Forest in November, 1983. However, he wanted to talk to his legal advisor/agent before signing on the dotted line. I came up with a plan and spoke to Derek Dougan at Wolves. We would sign Andy on loan, technically for 24 hours, which enabled us to beat the 5pm Thursday deadline. This gave Andy the extra time he needed and we were then able to complete everything on the Friday. The League later blocked this type of loophole, but it allowed us to tie things up and get him in the team for a game that we won 1-0 with a goal from Adrian Heath. Let's just say it was the start of something very special.

GARY LINEKER:

When you win the League Championship, your first instinct as a manager should be to go out and improve further. You can't sit back on your laurels. This is why I signed Gary Lineker from Leicester City in time for the 1985/86 season. Andy Gray had done a fantastic job for us, but I just felt it was time to inject a bit more pace up front, especially away from home.

Gary was a proven goalscorer and he was very quick. Other clubs were in for him, but he was ready to sign for us although a transfer tribunal would settle the fee. Gordon Milne, the former Liverpool player, was at Leicester and even though the fee came out at £800,000 with extras if sold on, he was clearly disappointed to be losing the lad.

I always remember his words after it was all done. He said: "You don't know what you've got."

Clearly, Gordon rated Lineker highly. When the player eventually started to work with us, he didn't knock the door down. He quietly got on with it, but the goals were soon mounting up and Milne's words were ringing true.

However, the pattern of our play was also changing because of Gary's style. Where previously the goals were coming from all areas of the field with five lads in double figures, the vast majority of our goals were now coming from Gary.

He finished up with 40, which is an astonishing return. It included an FA Cup Final goal against Liverpool, but we lost that match and were edged out in the fight to retain the title.

We were faced with a very difficult decision at the end of the season. The lad's personal haul had been magnificent, but I went to the directors and said: "I want to get back to the way we were in terms of pattern."

We didn't need to sell him for the money. It was linked with tactics. As it turned out, with Derek Mountfield injured, I found myself investing £900,000 in Dave Watson, but that was not directly linked with the Lineker sale to Barcelona, which generated £2.5 million.

It might have seemed strange to some Evertonians that we were prepared to unload the man who had just won the Golden Boot for his England goals in the 1986 World Cup, but it proved the right decision. The following year, with the goals shared out, we won the League again.

I should add that Terry Venables, then manager of Barcelona, wanted Gary before the World Cup. He was a bit shocked that we agreed and asked: "Why are you selling him?" as if there was some ulterior motive, other than tactics. I'm sure Terry wondered whether he was carrying some hidden injury or whether there was another reason. There wasn't.

Looking back, I just wish that we had secured an option to buy Gary back after his experience in Spain. He was still a very good player and did well for Tottenham when he eventually returned to England.

Certainly, no one can question Lineker for his return in 1985/86. I just believed in a wider goal contribution from the team. No disrespect to him whatsoever. He was a tremendous professional whose goal tally still speaks for itself.

PAUL WILKINSON:

When Grimsby came to Goodison in November 1984, their centre-forward Paul Wilkinson left us all with food for thought when he knocked us out of the League Cup with a goal in the very last minute. He was tall and clearly knew where the goal was and so I checked him out further, eventually signing him for £250,000.

 The amazing thing about the Grimsby game was that we were magnificent, but just couldn't score. It's not often you suffer at the hands of giant killers and still get a standing ovation going off the field. When I eventually signed Paul, I said to the staff: "There's one thing for sure. He won't be scoring a shock goal against us again!"

  Of course, by the end of the season, our fans were singing his name when he scored a famous winner in the Merseyside derby against Liverpool. Paul could not truly establish himself, not least because of the competition from the likes of Gary Lineker and Graeme Sharp, but he made enough appearances to secure a Championship medal in 1986/87 and I think he finished with 14 goals in 25 appearances which is a decent return before we recouped our money when we transferred him to Nottingham Forest.

WAYNE CLARKE:

Wayne was a talented player, but he wasn't fully appreciated by the fans, even at Birmingham where I signed him from. Sometimes that's not a good sign. When you go to watch a player, you sometimes mingle with the supporters because they are good judges and instinctively say what they think.

 I recognised an ability in him and hoped he would win the Everton fans over. He averaged a goal every other game in the ten matches he played from the March to the May as we clinched the 1987 title, including a hat-trick against Newcastle. He never fully convinced the Goodison faithful, but his fellow players recognised that he had something about him.

 One game I remember was at Arsenal towards the end of March where we won 1-0. Wayne chipped the keeper for the winner.

 I went to see Phantom of the Opera that night in the capital. Sarah Brightman was the big star. I think it was her last night and she got a standing ovation. The only thing I could think of was the standing ovation our lads had received a few hours earlier at Highbury. That result convinced me we could go on and win our second Championship.

 Wayne, of course, came from a famous football family. His elder brothers Alan and Frank, were both good players, particularly Alan who was a goalscoring idol at Leeds.

ANDY KING:

Not many London lads come up north and settle straight away. Andy immediately became an adopted Scouser when he joined Everton. He had great ability and the fans immediately took to him. He loved Everton Football Club.

Andy was originally signed by Billy Bingham in from Luton in 1976 for £35,000. He then joined Tommy Docherty's QPR in 1980 for £450,000 so the Blues got good value. Within 12 months he had moved to West Brom, but he had problems and in the July of 1982 he sought permission to train with us at Bellefield during the pre-season work. The more I looked at him and saw his infectious enthusiasm and ability, the more I thought he could improve us. I set up a straight swap deal with Peter Eastoe going to the Hawthorns.

Andy was thrilled when I decided to sign him and started the first 17 games that season. He was then out for spell, but returned to the side in late December to play some tremendous football. Probably, he was playing as well as he had ever done at that time until he suffered a terrible injury at Sunderland. He had scored about nine goals for us and the injury was a real blow.

It ruled Andy out for the remainder of the season which took us into that eventful 1983/84 year when everything began to take off. He actually started back in the team that season and was in the picture until the turn of the year.

I know how disappointed he was that he could not play a major part in our twin Wembley runs. He was actually sub in the Milk Cup Final. I know how bitterly disappointed he must have been because he was a good player and an excellent finisher. But he never quite recovered from that injury at Sunderland and moved on to play in Holland.

NEIL ADAMS:

Neil was a reasonable winger, but he lacked experience when we first signed him from Stoke. He had the unfortunate experience of being the first substitute to be subbed at Wembley! It was in the Charity Shield against Liverpool and I told him to go out there and help stop their left-back bombing down the line.

Neil was all over the place and I had no choice. I said: "Get him off." He was the most surprised person in the stadium, because a sub doesn't normally expect to be replaced.

When his number went up, he was standing there looking to see who was coming off. Even then he had to look over his shoulder to check it was his number that was up! It shows how much we wanted to win every game - even the Charity Shield that some people looked on as a showpiece.

KEVIN LANGLEY:

With all the injury problems we had going into the 1986/87 season, you tend to look at players in the lower divisions who you feel might have a chance. You are not going to be successful with all of them, but I watched Kevin a few times at Wigan. He was technically very good in midfield and obviously stood out at that level where he was comfortable on the ball.

You could take a chance at that level because you were not spending fortunes. Looking at weaknesses, possibly he wasn't the quickest, but then neither was Alan Harper and I signed him three times! I also signed another Wigan player, striker Warren Aspinall. When I saw Warren, I felt he might be the next Mark Hughes. It's only when you work with people that you really gain an understanding into their true strengths and weaknesses. I sold Aspinall to Aston Villa and made a profit, so that was fine.

Langley actually played in the opening 16 games at the start of that 1986/87 season and so ultimately qualified for a title medal, But when we were at full strength, we had better options and he too moved on fairly quickly.

ALAN IRVINE:

Alan Irvine is well known, and respected these days, as David Moyes' trusted assistant. He was actually Gordon Lee's last signing for Everton. Alan was in that mould of the traditional Scottish winger with the natural skill to go past his marker. This was linked with ability rather than pace. He was not a flying winger. Alan was a quiet lad who was never going to come hammering on your door if things were not going his way. He just got on with it. He was clearly an intelligent lad and he has made his mark as a coach. I know he is highly rated in the modern game which is why David Moyes put his faith in him when he was looking for a right hand man.

TERRY CURRAN:

Terry Curran was another extremely skilful winger. We took him on a successful loan spell from Sheffield United in 1982/83 when we needed a lift and he caught the mood of the fans. Eventually we made it permanent. Well, as permanent as it could be with Terry. He was one of the most travelled players in the game, turning out for the likes of Doncaster, Nottingham Forest, Bury, Derby, Southampton, Sheffield Wednesday, Sheffield United, Huddersfield, Panionis, Hull, Sunderland, Grantham, Grimsby and Chesterfield.

I needed someone with the confidence to hold the ball. As we battled for form, too many were shying away from it. When one player suddenly wants it, it's amazing how it can rub off on the others.Terry would play in our FA Cup semi-final win over Southampton at Highbury in 1984, but I didn't select him for the Final and he only made another handful of starts before resuming his travels.

Scroll of fame

Howard **Kendall**
Sir Philip **Carter**
Bill **Kenwright**
Jim **Greenwood**
Kevin **Abbot**
Tony **Aguiar**
I T **Allen**
Kevin **Alliston**
Michael **Ambrose**
Peter **Anders**
Colin **Armstrong**
John **Armstrong**
Martin J **Ashton**
Mally **Aspinall**
Edward **Austin**
Jon **Ballardie**
Alan **Barnes**
Ian **Bartley**
Mel **Basnett**
Francis William **Bates**
Alan **Bedford**
Andrew **Beesley**
Paul **Beesley**

Thomas Steven **Bell**
Graham **Bethell**
William Peter **Birch**
Kevin **Birchall**
Michael **Blackburn**
James **Boardman**
Tom **Bodden**
Joe **Boden**
John Charles **Bohanna**
Bill **Bracewell**
Daniel **Brennan**
Mark **Bretherton**
David **Briscoe**
Alex **Brooks**
Ian **Brooks**
Lee A **Brooks**
Simon A **Brooks**
Gavin **Buckland**
James **Bugden**
Frank **Burgess**
Stephen **Burke**
Stewart **Burns**
Mr Alfie **Buxton**

Barry **Byrne**
Mike **Byrne**
Mr Gerard Vincent **Cahill**
David **Calver**
Lorraine **Case**
Billy **Cassidy**
George **Caton**
Terry **Cavanagh**
Gary A **Chambers**
Ian **Chapman**
David **Charnock**
Richard **Chesters**
Mark **Clack**
Michael **Clack**
Andrew **Cobham**
Colin **Code**
Gerard **Coffey**
Stephen T **Cole**
Alun Thomas **Comer**
Paul **Condron**
Denis **Connor**
Jimmy **Connor**
Kevin **Conway**

Calum **Cooke**
Steven **Cooke**
David James **Coolican**
Christopher **Cooper**
John **Costello**
Michael **Cox**
Christopher **Coxon**
Liam **Coyle**
Andrew **Coyne**
Tommy **Creamer**
Mr Paul **Crilly**
Terry **Crosby**
Derek **Crotty**
Sean **Cuddihy**
Lawrence **Cuddy**
Paul **Cushion**
Andrew **Cushion**
Michelle **Daly/Finney**
Peter **Dalton**
Tanya **Danielle**
John **Davies**
Mark **Davies**
Martyn **Davies**
Ray **Davies**
Sion Huw **Davies**
John **Dean**
Callum **Deegan**
Ronnie **Deegan**
Tracey **Derbyshire**
Arthur **Dermott**
Brad **Dermott**

Peter **Dewhurst**
Barry **Dickens**
Siobhan **Dickson**
John 'Dohead' **Doherty**
Gary A **Donnelly**
David **Doran**
Frank **Dorman**
William **Douglas**
Michael **Driscoll**
John Anthony **Dunleavy**
Peter Paul **Dunne**
Gerard **Durham**
Paula **Durham**
Carl **Dyke**
Kevin **Edgar**
Edwards Jnr
Mark Henry Dominic **Ellis**
Mathew J **Ellis**
Robert D **Ellis**
Garry **Ellman**
Joseph **Ennis**
Anthony **Evans**
Geoffrey H **Evans**
Wayne J **Evans**
Tim 'Charlie' **Farley**
Christian **Fearnehough**
Mark **Fearnehough**
Richard **Fearnett**
Roy T **Fenton**
Frank **Finn**
Barry **Finnan**

The **Finneys**
Gary J **Firman**
James W **Firman**
Bernard J **Flood**
Stephen **Fogg**
Greg **Foley**
Steve **Foley**
Alan Samual **Fullard**
Ken **Gane**
Steven **Garner**
Daniel J **Gibson**
Harry **Gilgrist**
Stephen **Gilmore**
Charles **Gorton**
Gerard **Grace**
Louise **Grace**
Richard **Grace**
Chris **Greaves**
Anthony **Greenwood**
Mr Elfyn Wynne **Griffith**
Matthew **Griffiths**
Brian **Hall**
Dave **Hall**
Adrian **Halstead**
Gordon Noel **Hamilton**
Lucy Olivia **Handley**
John **Hankinson**
Angela **Hanrahan**
Nicola **Hanrahan**
John **Harding**
Neil **Hardiman**

Mark **Harpur**
Jimmy **Harrison**
Steven **Harrison**
Alan **Hartley**
Francine **Harty**
Anthony **Hatch**
Graham Brian **Hawes**
Phillip **Hayes**
Brian **Helm**
Susan **Henry**
Derek **Heron**
Andrew **Hilton**
Phil **Hilton**
Glen **Hind**
Michael **Hoban**
Peter **Holden**
Graeme **Holmes**
Frank **Howard**
Gary 'Buddy' **Howard**
John **Howard**
Lee **Howard**
Nick **Howard**
Chris **Hughes**
James Paul **Hughes**
James Pearson **Hughes**
Liam Gareth **Hughes**
Stephen **Hughes**
Steven **Hughes**
Kevin **Hutchinson**
John Richard **Ireland**
Joanne **Jackson**

Ian **Jarvis**
Philip David **Johnson**
Christopher David **Jones**
David James **Jones**
Gethin Wyn **Jones**
Graham **Jones**
Graham **Jones**
John **Jones**
Mr K P **Jones**
Neil Andrew **Jones**
Phil **Jones**
Stephen **Jones**
Steve 'Kipper' **Jones**
Thomas **Jones**
Danny **Kavanagh**
Vic **Kay**
Reg **Kearns**
Kevin **Keating**
Dave **Kelly**
Dave **Kelly**
Ian **Kemp**
John **Kenyon**
Richard Huw **Kerfoot**
Ian **Kidd**
Thomas **Kildare**
Paul **Kilroy**
Tony **Kirkham**
Liam **Kirwan**
Patrick **Kyle**
Walter **Langley**
Robert **Leatherbarrow**

Steven **Leonard**
Ryan **Lewin**
Alun **Lewis**
Mike **Lewis**
Richard **Liversey**
Paul **Livingstone**
John **Lloyd**
Billy **Long**
Colin **Lord**
Paul **Lowry**
Philip **Lowry**
Ronnie **Lunt**
Dennis **Macdonald**
Andy **Macrae**
Steven **Maguire**
Steve **Mahon**
Stuart **Makin**
Diane Marie **Malone**
Andrew **Maloney**
David **Manning**
Andrew **Marsh**
Jenna **Marsh**
Alan **Martin**
Philip **Martin**
Patrick Daniel **McCamley**
Sophie **McDonagh**
Lee **McDonnell**
Ian P **McDowall**
Kyle **McEllin**
Alan **McFarlane**
Mal **McFarlane**

Peter **McGimpsey**

Jamie **McKenzie**

Keith **McLeod**

John Michael **McLoughlin**

Phil J **McMaster**

Paul **McStein**

Alan **Medcalf**

Tom **Melia**

Gary George **Midford**

Crawford G **Miles**

Ern **Miles**

Scott A **Miles**

Mr Nick **Mitchelmore**

Kevin **Mohan**

Lisa **Mohan**

Paula **Mohan**

Bill **Moorcroft**

Brian **Morgan**

Thomas Stuart **Morgan**

Vivienne **Morgan**

John Joseph **Morley**

Dave **Morris**

Neil **Morris**

Paula **Mossford**

Liam **Mulcahy**

Tommy **Murray**

Jeff **Myers**

Alan **Mylett**

Stefan **Myszkowski**

Terry **Mythen**

Dave **Nation**

Gary **Naven**

Christopher J **Naylor**

Robert Eric **Nelson**

Andrew **Ness**

Andrew **Nicol**

Ian **Noon**

Peter **O'Connor**

Barry **O'Dwyer**

Daniel **O'Neil**

Simon Charles **O'Reilly**

Albert W **Orme**

Andrew A **Orme**

Philip **Orme**

Nigel **Orritt**

Andrew **Owen**

Barry **Owen**

Gareth **Owen**

Scott **Owen**

Steven K **Owen**

Bernard **Parker**

Thomas **Parker**

Ian **Parry**

Neil **Patten**

Thomas **Pinnington**

John R **Platt**

Ian **Povey**

Mark **Povey**

Stephen **Price**

Joe **Purcell**

Tony **Purcell**

Michael John **Quayle**

Robert **Quigley**

Phillip **Quinn**

Sarah Rosina **Radley**

John **Raftery**

Janet **Rainford**

Gary **Ratcliffe**

Phil **Ratcliffe**

Keith **Rens**

William Douglas **Richards**

Edward John **Riddell**

Lee **Rigby**

Hugh **Riley**

Hugh **Riley**

Thomas **Riley**

Ant **Rimmer**

Brian Geoffrey **Rimmer**

Peter P **Rimmer**

Ronald Geoffrey **Rimmer**

Andrew **Roberts**

Dafydd Hefin **Roberts**

Dave **Roberts**

Dave **Roberts**

John **Roberts**

Les **Roberts**

Peter **Rogers**

Ian **Ross**

Marian **Rothwell**

Hugh **Rule**

Mr D J **Ryan**

Alan **Sanderson**

Mr Jim **Saron**

Mr Michael **Saron**
Mike **Saunders**
William **Scaife**
Jack **Shaw**
Warren **Shaw**
Alec **Shields**
Nick **Shields**
David **Shone**
Philip **Shone**
Daniel **Simms**
Alan **Simpson**
Alan **Simpson** (MP)
Paul Richard **Simpson**
Lawrence J **Slaherty**
Lawrence M **Slaherty**
Michael D **Smith**
George **Smith** (NZ)
Hayley **Spencer**
Richard **Spencer**
Mark **Staniford**
David **Starsky**
Dave **Stowers**
Dave **Sumpter**
Peter **Sumpter**
Andrew James **Sutcliffe**
Louis **Tait**
Ian **Tandy**
Graham **Taylor**
Dave **Tickner**
Daniel **Tilley**
Paul **Tinsley**

Robert **Tomley**
Raymond **Trafford**
Colin **Trevitt**
Iain **Tucker**
Stuart **Tuffy**
David R **Tullitt**
Ian **Turnbull**
Frank Henry **Turpin**
Gareth **Turtle**
Keith **Turtle**
Michael **Turtle**
Lorraine **Tyrer**
Ranger Tony **Tyrer**
Matty **Vaudrey**
Billy **Vaughan**
Billy **Vaughan**
Lisa **Vaughan**
Ronald **Vaughan**
Andrew C **Vernon**
Dave **Vivane**
John **Waddington**
Eric **Wade**
Stuart **Wade**
Graham **Walker**
Andy **Wallace**
David **Wallis**
Sidney **Webb**
Daniel **Wells**
Paul Michael **West**
Paul **Wharton**
Anthony L **Wiggins**

Martin **Wilde**
Paula **Wilkinson**
Alan **Williams**
Gareth **Williams**
Geoff **Williams**
Harry **Williams**
Lee **Williams**
Mark **Williams**
Rachael **Williams**
Steve **Williams**
Mike **Wilson**
Ted **Wilson**
Jon **Winclebank**
Colin **Windrow**
Jimmy **Windrow**
Jason **Wright**
Steve **Wroldsen**